C000172304

Furness Iron

The Physical Remains of the Iron Industry and Related Woodland Industries of Furness and Southern Lakeland

Furness Iron

The Physical Remains of the Iron Industry and Related Woodland Industries of Furness and Southern Lakeland

edited by Mark Bowden

contributors

Amy Lax, Ian Goodall, Mark Bowden and Christopher Dunn

with other contributions by

Keith Blood, Keith Falconer and Colin Lofthouse

ENGLISH HERITAGE

Published by English Heritage at the National Monuments Record Centre,
Great Western Village, Kemble Drive, Swindon SN2 2GZ

Copyright © English Heritage 2000

Images (except as otherwise shown) © Crown copyright. NMR
Applications for the reproduction of images should be made to the
National Monuments Record

First Published 2000

ISBN 1 873592 47 7

Product Code XC20045

British Library Cataloguing in Publication Data
A CIP catalogue record for this book is available from the British Library

All rights reserved
No part of this publication may be reproduced or transmitted in any form
or by any means, electronic or mechanical, including photocopying,
recording, or any information storage and retrieval system, without
permission in writing from the publisher

Edited and indexed by Mike Ponsford
Designed by Mark Simmons, Eureka Projects!
Edited and brought to press by David M Jones, Andrew McLaren and
    Richard Jones, English Heritage

Printed by Snoeck-Ducaju & Zoon, Gent

Contents

Illustrations vi
Acknowledgements vii
Illustration acknowledgements vii
Summary viii
Résumé viii
Zusammenfassung ix

1 Introduction
The project 1
The geology and topography of Furness 4
A brief history of the industry 6

2 Raw Materials
Possible early iron ore extraction sites 12
Iron ore mines 14
Fluxes 21
Charcoal and related woodland industries 22

3 Processes
Transport 34
Bloomeries 37
Blast furnaces 44
Forges 65

4 Prospect 75

**Appendix: Management and
conservation by John Hodgson** 80

List of References 82

Index 85

Illustrations

Fig 1.1 Map showing sites and areas surveyed by the RCHME and other places mentioned in the text . facing page 1
Fig 1.2 The iron making process in Furness . 2
Fig 1.3 Duddon blast furnace – reconstruction drawing (LDNPA) 4
Fig 1.4 Low Furness – aerial photo 5
Fig 1.5 Nibthwaite – plan of 1746 8
Fig 1.6 Charcoal burners preparing the pit – drawing (A Heaton Cooper) 11
Fig 2.1 Urswick Stone Walls – plan 13
Fig 2.2 Bolton Heads – aerial photo 14
Fig 2.3 Subsidence at Park mines, Askham – 1930s photo (Frank Woodall) 15
Fig 2.4 Kathleen Pit, Roanhead – 1930s photo (Frank Woodall) 15
Fig 2.5 Nab Gill mine – plan 16
Fig 2.6 Stone Closes mine – plan 19
Fig 2.7 Pitsteads at Stony Hazel and Heald Wood – comparative plans 24
Fig 2.8 Potash kiln at Roudsea and comparative plans of bark-peelers' huts at Roudsea and Stony Hazel 25
Fig 2.9 Interior of a charcoal-burners' hut – drawing (A Heaton Cooper) 26
Fig 2.10 Bailiff Wood – plan 27
Fig 2.11 Bailiff Wood – detailed plan of pitstead and huts 29
Fig 2.12 Parrock Wood, Rigg Wood and Knott End Wood 30
Fig 2.13 Parrock Wood – detailed plan of pitstead, hut, and kiln 31
Fig 2.14 Roudsea Wood – plan 33
Fig 2.15 Roudsea, bark-peelers' hut – photo 34
Fig 2.16 Roudsea, bark barn – photo 35
Fig 3.1 Crane House Quay and Bigland Dock – plan 37
Fig 3.2 Crane House Quay – photo 38
Fig 3.3 Comparative plans of High Furness bloomeries 41
Fig 3.4 Tom Gill bloomeries – plan 44
Fig 3.5 Muncaster Head bloomforge – plan 45
Fig 3.6 Backbarrow Furnace – site plan 48
Fig 3.7 Duddon Furnace – buildings plan . 49
Fig 3.8 Duddon Furnace – photo 49
Fig 3.9 Newland Furnace – site plan 49
Fig 3.10 Nibthwaite Furnace – site plan 51
Fig 3.11 Duddon Furnace – water system plan 52
Fig 3.12 Duddon Furnace – 1890s photo .. 53

Fig 3.13 Duddon Furnace – photo 53
Fig 3.14 Nibthwaite Furnace – photo 54
Fig 3.15 Nibthwaite Furnace – plan and section 55
Fig 3.16 Nibthwaite Furnace – photo of furnace interior 56
Fig 3.17 Newland Furnace – plan and section 56
Fig 3.18 Duddon Furnace – photo of furnace interior 57
Fig 3.19 Newland Furnace – photo of c 1897 (North Lonsdale Magazine) 57
Fig 3.20 Backbarrow Furnace – photo of furnace stack 58
Fig 3.21 Leighton Furnace – drawing of ore store (Cumbria Record Office) 59
Fig 3.22 Newland Furnace – ore store plan and section 60
Fig 3.23 Backbarrow Furnace – photo of ore store and coke stores (Andrew Lowe) ... 60
Fig 3.24 Duddon Furnace – ore store plan and section 60
Fig 3.25 Nibthwaite Furnace – photo of charcoal barn (Mike Davies-Shiel) 61
Fig 3.26 Backbarrow Furnace – charcoal barn plan and section 62
Fig 3.27 Duddon Furnace – development diagram of charcoal barns 63
Fig 3.28 Duddon Furnace – photo of interior of charcoal barn 63
Fig 3.29 Newland Furnace – development diagram of charcoal barns 63
Fig 3.30 Newland Furnace – rolling mill/blacking mill plan 64
Fig 3.31 Duddon Furnace – photo of housing 65
Fig 3.32 Nibthwaite Furnace – photo of housing 66
Fig 3.33 Newland Furnace – photo of housing 67
Fig 3.34 Backbarrow Furnace – aerial photo 69
Fig 3.35 Hacket Forge – plan 70
Fig 3.36 Stony Hazel Forge – plan 73
Fig 3.37 Interior of a forge – illustration by Denis Diderot (Gillespie 1959, plate 95) 74
Fig 3.38 Stony Hazel Forge – photo 74
Fig 3.39 Stony Hazel – forge and plan 76
Fig 4.1 Roanhead – aerial photo 78
Fig 4.2 Charcoal burners – drawing (A Heaton Cooper) 80
Fig 4.3 Newland – photo 80

Acknowledgements

This project, undertaken by the Royal Commission on the Historical Monuments of England, was initially set up by Humphrey Welfare and latterly managed by Paul Everson. The fieldwork was undertaken by the contributors. The drawings have been prepared for publication by Allan Adams and Philip Sinton. Ground photographs were taken by Keith Buck and Roger Thomas and aerial photographs by Peter Horne and David MacLeod.

The RCHME is grateful to all the landowners, tenants and farmers who allowed access to their land and buildings, and to the following who assisted in many respects: Justine Bayley; David Cranstone; Peter Crew; David Crossley; Bette Hopkins (Cumbria SMR); Andrew Lowe and John Hodgson (Lake District National Park Authority); Dr John Marshall; Robert Maxwell (National Trust); Gerry McDonnell and other members of the Historical Metallurgy Society; Dr Marilyn Palmer; Anton Thomas (Cumbria Amenity Trust Mining History Society); Hilary Tidswell (SEARCH); Dr John Todd (Cumberland and Westmorland Antiquarian and Archaeological Society); Robert White.

Grants towards the costs of publication from the Cumberland and Westmorland Antiquarian and Archaeological Society and from the Lake District National Park Authority are gratefully acknowledged.

Illustration Acknowledgements

Permission to produce various figures has been given by the following individuals and institutions: the LDNPA (Fig 1.3); the Heaton Cooper Studio, Grasmere (Figs 1.6, 2.9, and 4.2); Mr Frank Woodall (Figs 2.3 and 2.4); Mrs Meryl Barker of Broughton-in-Furness (Fig 3.12); Cumbria Record Office, Barrow (Fig 3.20); Mr Andrew Lowe (Fig 3.22); Mr Mike Davies-Shiel (Fig 3.24); Fig 1.5 is reproduced from Brydson (1908), Fig 3.19 from the North Lonsdale Magazine 1897, and Fig 3.37 from Diderot's Encyclopaedia (Gillespie 1959, plate 95). All other illustrations are © Crown copyright.NMR.

Summary

The district of Furness and surrounding parts of southern and western Cumbria had a flourishing iron industry in the 18th and 19th centuries, growing out of a tradition of ironworking stretching back at least to the medieval period. The effects of this industry are still apparent in the landscape.

The Furness peninsula and adjacent coastal plain of southern Cumbria is a glacial landscape overlying sandstone and limestone formations containing significant deposits of high grade hematite iron ore. This mineral resource has probably been exploited from a very early period in the human occupation of the area and certainly since the medieval period. The northern hinterland of the Furness Fells, formed of volcanic rocks, shales and slates, supports extensive broad-leaved woodland which provided the charcoal necessary for smelting the iron. Among the fells are numerous fast-flowing becks and rivers, which enabled water power to be applied to the ironmaking process in later times. With the introduction of blast-furnace technology from 1711, the industry grew in importance through the 18th and 19th centuries.

The physical remains of this significant iron industry and its related woodland industries – earthworks, buildings and the surviving woodlands themselves – are well known locally but, until recently, have been relatively poorly recorded and have not taken their due place in national and international discussions of the history of ironworking. As a response to this situation, the Royal Commission on the Historical Monuments of England (now part of English Heritage) surveyed a representative sample of these remains between 1994 and 1999.

The project involved earthwork survey and landscape analysis, building survey and both ground and aerial photography. The sites, landscapes and buildings recorded related to the extractive process, transport, industrial processes and the social infrastructure – including mines, tracks, quays, charcoal pitsteads, potash kilns, bloomeries, blast furnaces, forges, woodsmen's huts and workers' housing. The results are summarised in this volume and the plans, reports and photographs are all available for consultation in the National Monuments Record.

This survey – in tandem with previous and concurrent studies by other organisations and individuals – has promoted the academic understanding of these industries and will also aid the sympathetic management and conservation of individual monuments and landscapes.

Résumé

Le district de Furness et les régions environnantes du sud et de l'ouest du comté de Cumbria avaient une industrie du fer florissante aux dix-huitième et dix-neuvième siècles, elle avait ses racines dans une tradition de travail du fer qui remontait au moins jusqu'à l'époque médiévale. Les effets de cette industrie sur le paysage sont toujours visibles.

La péninsule de Furness et la plaine côtière de la Cumbria du sud qui lui est adjacente consistent en un paysage glaciaire recouvrant des formations de grès et de calcaire contenant des dépôts significatifs de minerai de fer à haute teneur en hématite. Ces ressources en minerai ont probablement commencé à être exploitées à une période très précoce de l'occupation humaine de la région, et le sont certainement depuis la période médiévale. Au nord, l'arrière-pays des crêtes de Furness, formé de roches volcaniques, de schistes et d'ardoises, est couvert en grande partie de forêts de feuillus qui ont fourni le charbon de bois nécessaire à la fonte du fer. Parmi les roches coulent de nombreux ruisseaux et rivières aux cours rapides, qui permirent plus tard d'utiliser l'énergie hydraulique dans le procédé de fabrication du fer. Avec l'introduction de la technologie des hauts fourneaux à partir de 1711, l'industrie prit de l'importance tout au long des dix-huitième et dix-neuvième siècles. Les vestiges matériels de cette industrie sidérurgique significatrice et des industries forestières qui lui sont associées – les talus, les bâtiments et les forêts restantes elles-mêmes – sont bien connus localement mais, jusqu'à une époque récente, ils n'ont été qu'insuffisamment enregistrés et n'ont pas occupé la place qui leur est dûe dans les discussions nationales et internationales sur l'histoire du travail du fer. En réponse à cette situation, la Commission Royale pour les Monuments Historiques d'Angleterre (qui fait maintenant partie d'English Heritage) a organisé l'étude d'un échantillon représentatif de ces vestiges entre 1994 et 1999. Cette étude a inclus un relevé des talus et une analyse du paysage, un relevé des bâtiments, et des photographies à la fois au sol et aériennes. Les sites, les paysages et les bâtiments enregistrés avaient un rapport avec le procédé d'extraction, le transport, les procédés industriels et l'infrastructure sociale – ils comprennent des mines, les voies, des quais, des sites de meules, des fours à potasse, des fours à loupes, des hauts fourneaux, des forges, des cabanes de bûcherons et des logements pour les ouvriers. Les résultats sont résumés dans ce volume, et les plans, rapports, photographies peuvent être consultés aux archives des Monuments Nationaux.

Cette étude – en conjonction avec les recherches précédentes et concurrentes d'autres organisations et individus – a oeuvré en faveur de la promotion et de la compréhension académique de ces industries et facilitera également la gestion éclairée et la conservation de monuments et de paysages particuliers.

Traduction: Annie Pritchard

Zusammenfassung

Der Furnessdistrikt und die umlegenden Gegenden von Süd- und West-Cumbria hatte eine florierende Eisenindustrie im achtzehnten und neunzehnten Jahrhundert, gewachsen aus einer Eisenbearbeitung, welche bis ins Mittelalter streckt. Die Effekte dieser Industrie sind heute noch in der Landschaft erkennbar.

Die Furnesshalbinsel und die angefügte Küstenebene von Süd-Cumbria ist eine eiszeitliche Landschaft liegend über Schichten von Sand- und Kalkstein, reich an an hochgradigem Eisenerz. Diese Rohstoffquelle wurde wahrscheinlich schon seit sehr frühen menschlichen Zeiten, jedoch mit Gewissheit seit dem Mittelalter genutzt. Das nördliche Hinterland von Furness Fells, geformt aus vulkanischem Gestein und Schiefer, unterstützt weite Laubwälder, welche die notwendige Holzkohle zum Schmelzen des Eisens lieferten. Zwischen den Bergen sind zahlreiche Bäche und Flüsse, welche den Einsatz von Wasserkraft in der Eisengewinnung in späteren Jahren ermöglichte. Mit der Einführung von Hochofentechnologie in 1711 wuchs die Bedeutung dieser Industrie im achtzehnten und neunzehnten Jahrhundert. Die Überreste dieser wichtigen Industrie, Erdarbeiten, Gebäude und die Wälder selbst, sind lokal gut bekannt, aber bis vor Kurzem relativ schlecht aufgezeichnet und haben nicht den ihnen gebührenden Platz in den nationalen und internationalen Diskussionen über die Geschichte der Eisenbearbeitung bekommen. Als Antwort zu dieser Situation, untersuchte die Königliche Kommission für die Historischen Monumente Englands (jetzt Teil der English Heritage) einen repräsentativen Teil dieser Überreste zwischen 1994 und 1999. Das Projekt beinhaltete Erdarbeitenvermessungen, eine Landschaftsanalyse, Gebäudegutachten und Boden- und Luftfotografien. Die untersuchten Standorte, Landschaften und Gebäude sind verbunden mit der Eisengewinnung, dem Transport, den industriellen Prozessen und der sozialen Infrastruktur – eingenommen der Minen, Wege, Stege, Holzkohlegruben, Schmelzen, Hochöfen, Schmieden, Holzarbeiterhütten und Arbeiterhäuser. Die Resultate sind in diesem Volumen zusammen gefaßt und die Pläne, Studien und Fotografien sind alle zur Beratung von den Nationale Monumente Aufzeichnungen (National Monuments Records) erhältlich.

Diese Untersuchung – in Tandem mit früheren und gleichzeitigen Studien bei anderen Organisationen und Einzelpersonen – hilft dem akademischen Verständnis dieser Industrien und dem gefühlvollen Management und Erhaltung von individuellen Monumenten und Landschaften.

Übersetzung: Norman Behrend

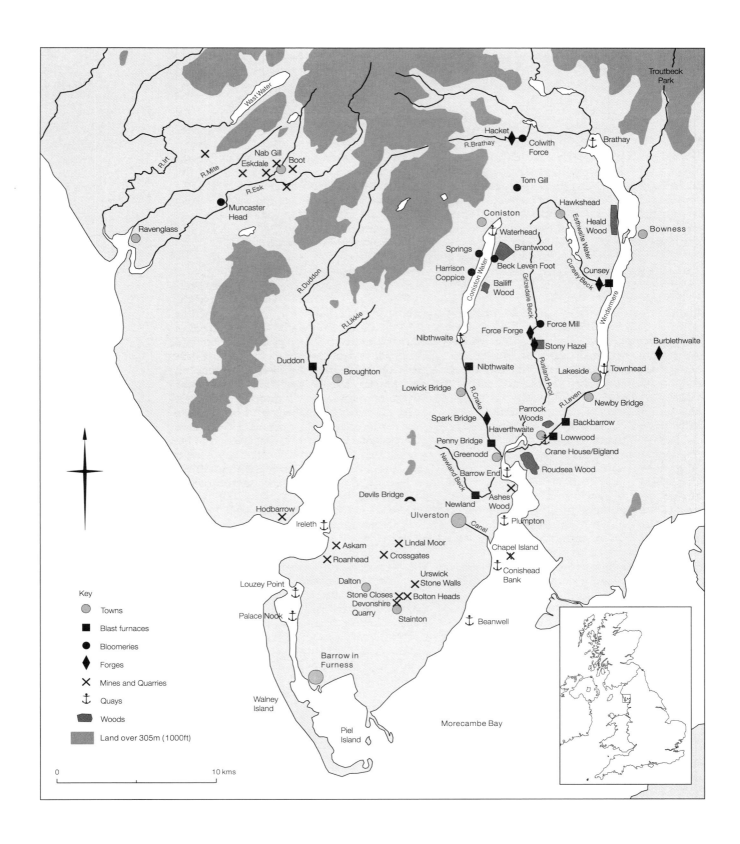

Key

- ⬤ Towns
- ■ Blast furnaces
- ● Bloomeries
- ◆ Forges
- ✕ Mines and Quarries
- ⚓ Quays
- Woods
- Land over 305m (1000ft)

Troutbeck Park

Hacket
R.Brathay
Colwith Force
Brathay

Wast Water

Nab Gill
Eskdale
Boot
✕

R.Mite
R.Irt
R.Esk

Muncaster Head

Ravenglass

Tom Gill

Hawkshead
Heald Wood
Esthwaite Water
Bowness

Coniston
Waterhead
Springs
Brantwood
Beck Leven Foot
Harrison Coppice
Bailiff Wood
Cunsey
Cunsey Beck

Coniston Water
Grizedale Beck
Windermere

Force Mill
Force Forge
Stony Hazel

Nibthwaite
Burblethwaite

Nibthwaite
Lakeside
Townhead

R.Duddon

Duddon
Broughton

Lowick Bridge

R.Llkke

R.Crake
Rusland Pool
R.Leven
Newby Bridge

Spark Bridge
Parrock Woods
Backbarrow
Haverthwaite
Lowwood

Penny Bridge
Greenodd
Crane House/Bigland
Roudsea Wood

Newland Beck
Barrow End

Devils Bridge
Newland
Ashes Wood
Plumpton

Hodbarrow
✕
Ireleth
Ulverston
Canal

Askam
Lindal Moor
Crossgates
Roanhead

Louzey Point
Chapel Island
Conishead Bank

Dalton
Urswick Stone Walls

Stone Closes
Devonshire Quarry
Bolton Heads
Stainton
Beanwell

Palace Nook

Barrow in Furness

Walney Island

Piel Island

Morecambe Bay

0   10 kms

1
Introduction

The Project

The district of Furness and surrounding parts of southern and western Cumbria (Fig 1.1) had a lively and significant iron industry in the 18th and 19th centuries, which grew out of a tradition of ironworking stretching back to at least the medieval period. Despite the publication of a magisterial history of the industry by Alfred Fell in 1908 and the enthusiastic researches of local historians and archaeologists (for example Marshall 1958; McFadzean 1989), the significance of this industry has hardly gained public recognition regionally, let alone nationally, unlike the iron industries of the Weald (Cleere and Crossley 1995) and the Forest of Dean (Hart 1971), for instance. Certainly the physical remains of the Furness industry were poorly represented in the National Monuments Record (NMR) and a survey of these remains was overdue.

It was principally for this reason that in 1994 the Royal Commission on the Historical Monuments of England embarked on a project to record at least the better preserved and most representative relict sites and landscapes of the Furness iron industry. The purpose of such recording is twofold: to interpret and improve understanding of the physical remains and to provide information to those charged with managing and preserving the buildings, sites and landscapes as part of the historical environment (*see* Appendix).

The topic has not been entirely neglected however. For instance, much work has been done on the location of bloomery sites by Davies-Shiel (1998) and others. Other projects in the area which have had a bearing on the RCHME's work were running prior to and concurrently with this project. These include surveys by the Lancaster University Archaeological Unit on behalf of the Lake District National Park Authority (LDNPA); recording of the remains of iron mines in Low Furness by the Cumbria Amenity Trust Mining History Society; and a survey of former woodland in Troutbeck Park by the SEARCH group. In addition to these, geophysical surveys of some bloomery sites have been undertaken by John Price and Peter Crew on behalf of the LDNPA since the RCHME fieldwork ended.

It is clear that the iron industry of Furness was closely related to other aspects of the local woodland economy. Since the industry was charcoal based until a surprisingly late date (the blast furnace at Backbarrow did not convert to coke until 1921), it was necessary to record not only the iron mines and ironworking sites, but also the remains of the charcoal industry. Charcoal making was (and remains) a seasonal activity, however, and brings with it a number of other seasonal woodland crafts such as bark peeling, potash production and the management of the woodland itself. The remains of these industries, which represent other parts of the lives of the same people, could not be ignored.

Similarly, the project was not restricted to the area generally known as Furness, but took in, selectively, remains in south-western Cumbria and individual sites such as Leighton (SD 487 778) near Carnforth, which were historically connected to the charcoal-based Furness industry, although geographically outside the region.

Survey methodology

With limited time and resources it was clear that the RCHME could not record everything – Cumbria has one of the largest concentrations of bloomeries in Britain, for instance, many of which are in Furness. The project therefore began with an extensive phase of reconnaissance, the aim being to draw up a priority list of selected representative sites or those which were illustrative of a particular process.

Figure 1.1 (facing page) Map of southern Lakeland showing sites and areas surveyed by the RCHME and other places mentioned in the text.

The sites and areas selected were surveyed with a combination of electronic and traditional methods. A differential Global Positioning System by satellites (GPS) was tried out, but it was clear that, although it could supplement it could not effectively replace other survey methods in the predominantly wooded environment of Furness. It was not, therefore, extensively used in the project. Instead, more conventional co-axial Electronic Distance Measurement (EDM) was used for establishing control and surveying 'hard' detail (buildings, walls and so on). 'Soft' archaeological earthworks were surveyed into this control framework using plane table with self-reducing alidade and tape-and-offset methods. These techniques are generally found to be most effective for surveying subtle and complex archaeological earthworks, where interpreting and gaining an understanding of the remains – rather than simply making a record – is of paramount importance. In contrast to the hundreds of bloomeries (and possibly thousands of pitsteads), there were only ever eight blast furnaces. All were visited and, at the four where significant remains survive measured survey, photography and detailed investigation were carried out. Aerial photography is,

for obvious reasons, of limited use in wooded landscapes. Nevertheless, aerial reconnaissance was employed for recording and examining the mining sites of Low Furness and some of the architectural monuments of the industry.

Documentary research as part of this project was limited largely to secondary sources. Targeted, selective documentary research was undertaken to underpin what was primarily an investigation of the physical remains, but much historical research has already been done, particularly on the larger ironworking sites, often enough to provide a good background.

All survey plans and accompanying reports have been deposited in the NMR where they are available for public consultation. Those sites and areas not surveyed in detail were nevertheless archived in summary fashion on the NMR's computer database.

A note on terminology (Fig 1.2)

The technical language associated with the study of the early iron industry is often imprecise, obscure and disputed. This is not entirely due to the failings of modern scholarship, but reflects the reality that prevailed within the industry throughout

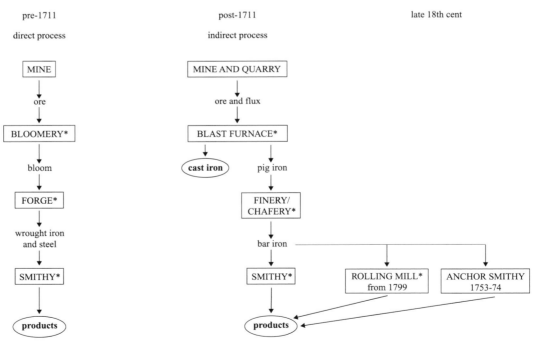

Figure 1.2 The iron making process in Furness.

* process using charcoal

Europe before the 19th century. Although the French, for instance, were at times leaders in the field of iron metallurgy, they had very few terms for describing the qualities of iron. Further, the limited scientific knowledge of ironmasters – even the most innovative – led them to use colloquial terms for their processes (Wertime 1962, 182, 227–32).

To this poverty of technical language further complications have to be added. First, there was great regional variation in terminology, such as the term 'ancony', which in Furness was apparently used to distinguish finery iron from bloomforge iron in the early 18th century (Fell 1908, 250). Second is the fact that those engaged in small-scale industry, especially one in which some of the processes could be described as a 'capricious art' (Wertime 1962, 181), rarely found it either possible or necessary to describe their processes in writing. It is, therefore, perhaps unsurprising that historians of the industry cannot agree over the precise meanings of terms such as 'bloomsmithy' and 'bloomforge'. The following paragraphs present a brief discussion of some of the more problematic and frequently found terms.

A **bloomery** was a charcoal-fired furnace for the direct reduction of iron ore to produce a 'bloom', usually a spongy mass of wrought iron or – occasionally – steel; the bellows of a bloomery may be manual or water powered. The bloom must be hammered and reheated in a forge, which might or might not be on the same site, to drive out any remaining slag and other impurities. The forge hammer, where present, could be operated manually by a treadle or by water power. Most bloomeries had one hearth for smelting and for reheating if required; in a bloomery which incorporated a second forging hearth, that hearth was referred to as a **stringhearth**. In addition to its particular meaning, 'bloomery' is also used by many authors as a general term for a variety of sites including bloomsmithies and bloomforges.

Bloomsmithy is a term for a combined bloomery and forge with only one hearth, but with both the bellows and the hammer water-driven. Most writers about the Furness industry restrict this term to 16th-century sites, although some use it more broadly to cover sites which others call **bloomforges** or bloomery forges – direct

smelting sites which continued in use at the same time as the indirect process of iron manufacture, and which may not have differed substantially from the finery and chafery forges of the indirect process (Awty and Phillips 1980, 25). In Furness this term seems to have been in use in the 17th century and into the early 18th century.

The **blast furnace** (charcoal-fired in Furness; Fig 1.3) was for the indirect process of reducing iron ore to cast iron, a technology introduced to Britain in the 15th century. The temperature was raised by water-driven bellows to produce an alloy of iron and carbon which can be run off in liquid form into an elongated mould with side branches in a sand bed, reminiscent of a sow and her litter; the resulting 'sow' and 'pigs' of brittle cast iron were then taken to be forged into malleable or wrought iron. Alternatively, objects could be cast directly into moulds. Wertime (1962, 45) has commented on the gradual transition from the direct process bloomery, which may explain why the cast-iron-producing furnace came to be known by the 'undistinguishing' terms 'blast furnace' (English) or 'high furnace' (German, French, Italian). This 'gradual' transition is also manifested physically in the forges of the early blast furnace era.

Cast-iron pigs from the blast furnace were taken to the **finery**, a charcoal-fired forge, usually water-powered, where pig iron was converted to wrought iron by reheating gradually to burn out the carbon. It was then hammered into an ancony before being reheated and forged into wrought iron bars in a **chafery** hearth, another charcoal-fired forge, usually water powered. These wrought-iron bars were then suitable for reworking into finished products. Finery and chafery could be, and apparently often were, under one roof; in the 19th century, the Swedish iron industry employed a 'Lancashire forge', an enclosed finery-and-chafery, apparently modelled on one observed by the Swedish metallurgist Gustaf Ekman near Ulverston (Trinder 1992, 393).

Even if agreement could be reached concerning this terminology, it is often extremely difficult to distinguish the remains of the different types of processing plant and impossible to date them by surface observation alone; even excavation may not reveal enough information to make a confident classification. This is equally

*Figure 1.3
Duddon blast
furnace:
reconstruction
(drawn by Alison
Whitby for
LDNPA).*

true of slags, which are sometimes said to be inherently dateable; the variation in slag produced at different stages in a single smelting or refining operation renders this impossible, although some technological identification is possible at a basic level. Some writers have made bold statements about the date and type of remains that they have observed, but such claims should be treated with caution.

The geology and topography of Furness

Furness comprises two contrasting regions, High and Low (or Plain) Furness. High Furness is the upland area defined by Windermere to the east, the rivers Duddon to the west and Brathay to the north, while Low Furness is the lowland peninsula to the south (Fig 1.4). In addition, this project has – selectively – taken in the remains of the iron industry in neighbouring districts. Furness now lies entirely within Cumbria. Historically, however, the region was part of Lancashire, bordered by Westmorland to the north and Cumberland, including Eskdale, on the west. The old county boundaries were formed largely by the rivers Brathay and Duddon. The name Furness means 'Fouldray headland', Fouldray being the Old Norse name of Piel Island.

The fells of Eskdale and High Furness are formed by Ordovician volcanic rocks and, to the south, by Silurian shales and slates. They are cut by Windermere and Coniston Water and numerous valleys which drain into the Esk, the Duddon and Morecambe Bay. The higher ground (above 300m OD) is characterised by rock outcrops, tarns and becks, and is currently heathland and rough grazing, while the lower slopes support extensive mixed deciduous woodland with some conifer plantations and permanent pasture. Behind the intertidal flats and sand dunes of the Esk and Duddon estuaries and Morecambe Bay are low undulating hills formed from glacial deposits, mainly boulder clay, overlying Triassic sandstones and Carboniferous limestones. The rounded slopes of the gentle hills are interrupted by numerous small crags. Limestone pavement is also found, as in the neighbourhood of Urswick. The present landscape is predominantly one of pasture with some woodland. It is here, in the limestones of the west coast and Low Furness, that the great hematite – iron ore – deposits lie.

Deposits of ore are found over a very large area of west and south-west Cumbria. The hematite in Low Furness is a rich, low phosphorus ore. It is a replacement deposit in the Carboniferous limestone, both in narrow veins and in massive orebodies which occur as 'flats' – tabular bodies – or 'sops' – inverted cones. These orebodies are irregular, however, differing greatly in shape and extent. Some lie at considerable depth, while many have been found near enough to the surface to be worked as open quarries. Most of the deposits are flat but vary in thickness from 1–2m to 70m or more. The largest deposit of ore, at Hodbarrow, was discovered by the appearance of veins on the shore – the greater part of the deposit was found to be under the sea. There are further large deposits at Askam, Roanhead and Lindal Moor, for example. Further descriptions of the ore can be found in *British Regional Geology: Northern England* (1971, 95), Fell (1908, 74–5, 88–90), Postlethwaite (1913, 140–7), Rose and Dunham (1977, 1–4) and Smith (1924).

Whether there was also bog ore in High Furness in sufficient quantity to be worked viably is not known, but it is a distinct possibility that some of the earlier bloomeries in the fells could have been exploiting localised deposits.

Figure 1.4
Piel Island, in the foreground, guards the entrance to Barrow harbour; the town of Barrow, developed by the ironmasters of Furness, lies at the end of the peninsula. Beyond it can be seen the Low Furness iron ore field and the Duddon estuary. In the distance are Black Combe and the fells between Dunnerdale and Eskdale (NMR 17190/46).

A brief history of the industry

Before the blast furnaces

The earliest known evidence for the exploitation of iron ore in Furness is a pair of Neolithic polished stone axes, one of them stained with hematite, which were discovered beside a hematite face in an old working at Stainton. Hematite was widely used in the Neolithic period as a pigment, probably for cosmetic and possibly symbolic body colouring; the very pure Furness ore would have been ideal for the purpose and therefore highly prized. The axes themselves may be best interpreted as a ritual deposit, a gift to the appropriate deity. A 'rude implement of iron' was also found nearby (Tweddell 1876, 38).

Thereafter, definite evidence for exploitation of the ore is lacking until the medieval period, although some of the extraction trenches and bloomeries might date to the Iron Age, Roman or Anglo-Saxon periods. It is almost inconceivable that this rich and often highly visible mineral was not exploited at these periods but, as Cowper put it, 'we have not one tittle of evidence that any hearths in the fells of Lancashire date from Roman or pre-Norman times' (1898, 101). Sadly that is still true in Furness one hundred years later, though bloomeries of these periods have been identified in other parts of the country.

That iron-ore mining in Furness had begun before 1086 is suggested by the mention of the name 'Orgrave' in Domesday Book, as noted tentatively by Fell (1908, 13). 'Grave' or 'groove' is a name frequently applied to sites of metallic ore extraction in the north of England. Mines at Orgrave, Elliscales, Marton and Plumpton are mentioned in documents of the 13th century but these seem to have been surface workings. Underground working is first suggested by the terms of documents referring to Marton at the end of the 14th century. Mines are not mentioned, however, in the Dissolution survey of Furness Abbey and there is little other mention of iron mining in Furness in the 16th and 17th centuries. There are references to iron processing at Mouzell, Ulverston and Newland in the 13th and 14th centuries. Furness Abbey seems to have secured the sole right to make iron in the district by 1273, but there is no evidence that the abbey sold or exported iron, the suggestion being that they only made enough for their own use and that of their tenants (Fell 1908, 14–31, 162–74). Alhough Collingwood certainly suggested that ironworks provided a major part of the abbey's income in the late 13th century (1902, 5–6), ironworking did not generally compare with sheep farming in the economic life of the abbey.

Some woodlands were being coppiced by at least the 14th century, both for charcoal burning and for the full range of other woodland industries – bark peeling, potash production, 'swill' basket making, turning and joinery (Winchester 1987, 104–5).

By the mid-16th century, and possibly before the Dissolution, ironmaking was in the hands of the Sandys and Sawrey families and, in the manor of Hawkshead, which covered most of High Furness, was apparently concentrated in three 'bloomsmithies', installations of more permanent character than the numerous bloomeries; the bloomsmithies were certainly water-powered, with smelting and forging taking place at the same location. They were located at Cunsey, at Force Mills and the third was probably somewhere near Backbarrow (Fell 1908, 178–90).

The bloomsmithies were abolished by a decree of Elizabeth I in 1564, ostensibly to protect the timber trees. Thereafter, iron production on a domestic scale only was permitted, using underwood and 'loppings' as fuel. This is one of many legal interventions and inquiries into the management of woodland throughout England in the later 16th and 17th centuries, suggesting that this period witnessed a low point in the history of woodland management, or at least that there was widespread concern about standards of woodmanship. In Furness it is tempting to suggest that this was due to ruthless exploitation of the woods by new entrepreneurs within the former estates of Furness Abbey following the Dissolution. There is no direct evidence for this, however, and similar explanations cannot hold for woodlands elsewhere in the country which had never been in monastic hands. The idea that ironmasters destroyed the woodlands of England between 1500 and 1700 has been firmly refuted, but that there was a perception that ironmasters were depriving others of previously cheap fuel seems to be reflected by the legislation; industries which relied on a plentiful supply of timber tended to protect woodland (Rackham 1990, 84–5).

Though there may have been local shortages of charcoal in Cumbria during the 17th century, wood supplies were generally more than adequate to meet the demands of the iron industry. Ore was so plentiful and conveniently located for shipping that, in addition to that being consumed by the local industry, much was being exported to distant smelting sites (Phillips 1977a, 4 and 25).

The later 16th century appears to have been a period of relatively little activity in the Cumbrian iron industry, but even though it remained small by national standards, production expanded through the 17th century. Perhaps significantly, the one securely archaeologically dated bloomery, at Muncaster Head, was operating during this time (Tylecote and Cherry 1970). Several other 'bloomforges' were in operation from the 1620s onwards, including Cunsey, Force Forge, Backbarrow, Hacket and Coniston. These all presumably used water power for hammers as well as for bellows. The output of the bloomforges was sold locally to smiths and ironmongers in Westmorland and northern Lancashire, but some was also shipped farther afield, for instance to Preston (Awty and Phillips 1980, 28).

The blast furnace era

The first blast furnace in Cumbria was built at Cleator on the west coast in 1694, but it was the early years of the 18th century which saw the introduction of blast furnace technology to Furness and the consequent demise of the bloomforge. Eight blast furnaces were built between 1711 and 1748, all of them charcoal fired and water powered, and they were established both by enterprising local families, some of them already involved with the existing iron industry, and by outsiders with interests in the iron trade of the West Midlands. (The principal sources for this section are Fell 1908; Marshall 1958, especially 19–41; Riden 1993.)

Construction of the first two blast furnaces, by the rival Backbarrow and Cunsey Companies, began in 1711.

The Backbarrow Company was led by two local ironmasters, John Machell and William Rawlinson, while the Cunsey Company was initially headed by Edward Hall and Daniel and Thomas Cotton, Cheshire ironmasters with interests in the West Midlands iron industry, who were attracted to Furness by the abundance of ore, charcoal and water, the last for both power and transport. The furnace at Backbarrow entered its first blast on 12 June 1712, a few months ahead of that at Cunsey. The Backbarrow Company immediately began to spread its operations by obtaining mining leases in Low Furness, buying up or leasing old bloomery forges, converting its own bloomforge to a finery forge and building a second blast furnace, at Leighton near Carnforth, in 1713. Its lease on the bloomforge at Cunsey, close to Cunsey Furnace, expired in 1715 and the site was then taken over by the Cunsey Company, which reconstructed it as a refinery and worked it in conjunction with their blast furnace. In 1715 the Cunsey Company also took over the forges at Coniston and Hacket jointly with their rivals, the beginning of a fruitful co-operation with the Backbarrow Company that was to last for many years. Jointly and separately these two companies set about acquiring mines and processing plants in such a way as to forestall any opposition. The new forge at Stony Hazel, for instance, was bought up by the Backbarrow and Cunsey Companies expressly to put it out of operation.

After the construction of Leighton Furnace in 1713, no moves were taken to establish further blast furnaces until the late 1720s and 1730s. In 1727 Thomas Rawlinson, eldest son of William Rawlinson of the Backbarrow Company, agreed to build Invergarry Furnace near Loch Garry in Inverness-shire. His partners in this Scottish venture were principally drawn from the Backbarrow Company, which supplied all the needs of the furnace except its charcoal. In 1728, back in Furness, an agreement to build a blast furnace at Lowwood, made between John Bigland, the landowner, and Richard Ford, manager of the Cunsey Company since 1718, came to nought. In 1735, however, Ford signed an agreement with Thomas Rigg of Nibthwaite Grange to build a blast furnace on the latter's estate just south of Coniston Water. Rigg recorded having 'a special Trust in the

Honesty of the said Richard Ford and his capacity to direct Iron Works' (Fell 1908, 211), and the furnace was built in 1735–6 (Fig 1.5). The construction of Nibthwaite Furnace coincided with the closure of Invergarry Furnace in 1736 as a commercial failure. This may have been one of the reasons which led the Backbarrow Company to set up a partnership with the Cunsey Company in March 1737 to build and operate Duddon Furnace. The consortium was, however, broken up in August 1741 when the Backbarrow partners assigned their moiety to those from Cunsey.

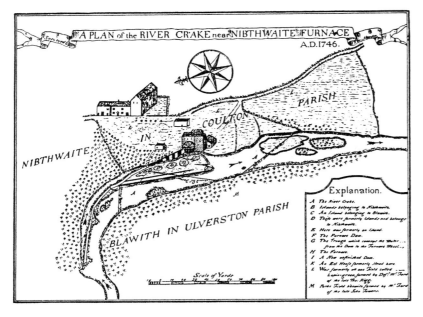

Figure 1.5 A plan of Nibthwaite Furnace, 1746 (Brydson 1908).

The late 1740s saw the construction of the last three blast furnaces, all of them built by men with links, albeit very different ones, with the existing industry. When Richard Ford's partnership with the Rigg family at Nibthwaite Furnace did not run smoothly, Ford determined to build a furnace in his own right. This he achieved with the construction of Newland Furnace in 1746–7, where the partnership agreement granted him sole management of the business, which was known as the Newland Company. Newland was six miles from Nibthwaite and, to avoid a clause which required him to give notice about his involvement in any other ironworks within ten miles, the lease of the site of Newland Furnace was taken in the name of his sister, Agnes Bordley. The last two blast furnaces were built at Lowwood and Penny Bridge. The attempt to build a furnace at Lowwood

in 1728 had foundered, but in 1747 it met with success, the partners in the Lowwood Company including Job Rawlinson and Isaac Wilkinson, whose fathers were associated with the industry. The founders of Penny Bridge Furnace also had connections with the iron industry, but of a different nature. 'Having just reason to apprehend a combination among the Ironmasters unreasonably to lower the price of Charcoal . . .' (Fell 1908, 221), a group of wood owners combined in 1748 under the leadership of William Penny to build their own blast furnace at Penny Bridge. Building began that year, but in 1749 the Backbarrow Company offered the promoters of the new furnace shares in its undertaking. The amalgamation was carried through and the object in building the new furnace was, therefore, to a great extent removed.

In 1749, a year after the construction of the last furnace, the Backbarrow, Cunsey and Newland Companies between them owned six of the eight blast furnaces in Furness.

Neither the number of furnaces nor their ownership remained static for long: within 40 years there were just four blast furnaces, a number reduced to one by the end of the 19th century and finally to none in 1966. Cunsey was the first blast furnace to close. Its lease and that of the associated forge ended in 1750 and, although the Backbarrow Company took them both over, neither was worked after that date. The furnace at Nibthwaite probably ceased to work after about 1755, the Newland Company concentrating its production of cast iron in Furness at Newland Furnace, although its forge at Nibthwaite continued in use until 1840. In 1755 the Backbarrow Company declined to renew its lease of Leighton Furnace. This was taken by the Halton Company of Lancaster, which ran it until about 1806. Penny Bridge Furnace, in which the Backbarrow Company had an interest, closed in 1780. As for the Lowwood furnace, although the Backbarrow and Newland Companies took the lease in 1782, they ran it for just three years before dismantling it. Their motives are clear from the fact that, when the lease expired in 1798, it was agreed with the owner that no furnace or forge would be worked on the premises during the next 15 years; in 1799 Lowwood Gunpowder Works was erected on the site. In 1818 Harrison,

Ainslie and Company, the successors of the Newland Company, bought the Backbarrow Company. They completed their monopoly in 1828 by buying Duddon Furnace. Duddon was closed in 1867 and Newland itself in 1891. Backbarrow continued in operation until 1966, having converted to coke in 1921. Since 1780, the company had been exploiting one of the finest natural harbours on the north-west coast by developing the new town of Barrow (Tweddell 1876, 260–1), where the massive iron and steel works which were to develop in the later 19th century would be coke fired.

The Scottish component of the Furness industry has already been seen in the establishment of the ill-fated Invergarry Furnace of 1727–36 by a scion of the Backbarrow Company. The availability of charcoal appears to have been the attraction, as it was in the 1750s when two further blast furnaces were built in Argyll. The Newland Company built Bonawe Furnace (also known as Lorn Furnace) in 1752–3, while Kendall and Latham of Duddon founded the Argyll Company and built Craleckan Furnace in about 1754. The latter ran until about 1813, primarily supplying the Kendalls' forge interests in the Midlands, while the former did not close until 1876.

Securing supplies of raw materials and fuel was of the utmost importance to the operators of the blast furnaces and their associated forges. All the companies acquired their own mines and the supply of ore was never a problem; indeed ore was still exported to other ironworking areas – Scotland, Wales, Dean, south Yorkshire and the Midlands – and the need to dispose of surpluses led in the 1760s to 'sales drives', the stockpiling of ore and the temporary closure of mines. Flux, a substance which promoted the elimination of non-metallic impurities, was also relatively easily obtained. Limestone was commonly used as a flux and was, of course, available in the same areas as the ore. Slag was often taken from old ironworking sites (rendering these sites more difficult to discover and to interpret) because it often contained more usable iron than some ores and was believed to have fluxing properties. Furnaces occasionally ran short of fuel, however, and were reduced to picking over their own slag heaps for unburnt charcoal and buying charcoal in lots as small as a single bag.

This was not due to a genuine shortage of coppice wood but, initially, to a shortage of manpower and to commercial pressures. Some labour was imported from other parts of Britain, not only to build the furnaces, forges and ancillary structures, but also to produce charcoal. From an early date, the ironmasters entered into agreements for the purchase of charcoal to keep prices down. The Backbarrow and Cunsey Companies initially competed for charcoal woods. This caused the price of wood to increase, but the intervention of the Shropshire ironmaster, Abraham Darby, in 1712 led to a price-fixing arrangement between the partnerships. The arrangements Richard Ford made to obtain charcoal at Nibthwaite and then Newland Furnaces are not known, but it would not have been in his interest either to drive up prices or create shortages. Wood owners not unnaturally objected to price fixing and, as noted above, a group of them combined in 1748 to establish their own blast furnace at Penny Bridge. This partnership was soon infiltrated by James Machell of Backbarrow, amalgamating the two companies in 1749 and leaving the Newland and Lowwood Companies out in the cold. There was some legal wrangling among the subscribers to the partnership, but in 1781, shortly after its 30-year term lapsed, the three surviving companies – Backbarrow, Newland and Lowwood – entered into a new agreement for the division of all the charcoal produced in the district. This continued in force until 1800, by which time the Lowwood Company had ceased to exist. The surviving companies reached a new understanding, which was respected until 1818 when the Backbarrow Company was taken over by Harrison, Ainslie and Company, as the Newland Company had become.

Like other British industries of the period, the Furness iron industry was almost totally reliant on local investment for its capital, although the Cunsey Company maintained its relationship, financial and otherwise, with the iron industry of the West Midlands. London financiers showed little interest in manufacturing industry and, outside London, banking was a late growth, leading to desperate shortages of cash for manufacturers throughout most of the 18th century (Ashton 1955, 173–86). The Furness iron companies therefore remained family businesses throughout their history, controlled by the Rawlinsons, the Machells, the Knotts, the Harrisons, the Ainslies and their partners and relatives. The iron companies themselves provided banking services in the later 18th century (Marshall 1958, 27–8).

Because the smelting furnaces of Furness remained charcoal-based long after coke had been adopted elsewhere, it is often seen as being an excessively conservative industry. In fact the Furness ironmasters had shown an interest in experimentation and innovation several times. As early as 1712, the Backbarrow Company had given samples of ore to Abraham Darby for experimental purposes and had themselves experimented with slag and ore from the Forest of Dean. Perhaps the most intriguing case, however, is that of Isaac Wilkinson. He was working as a 'pot-founder' at Backbarrow by 1740, where he developed the blowing cylinder and also patented improvements in foundry technology (Cranstone 1991) and was a partner in the Lowwood Company. In 1748 he moved to Wilson House, Lindale, where it has been claimed that he worked a blast furnace, but Cranstone has thrown doubt on this (ibid, 91). His son John moved to Staffordshire, later becoming a famous ironmaster. Experiments with peat firing were undertaken at Backbarrow in 1770 and at Newland in the 19th century (Marshall et al 1996), but ultimately the continued abundance of charcoal made such experiments unnecessary.

The products of the furnaces were principally pig iron which was either exported for use elsewhere – particularly south Wales and the Midlands – or converted in their own forges to bar iron. Many of these forges were short-lived. A refining forge was established at Backbarrow in 1712. Another refining forge opened at Nibthwaite Furnace in 1751 and, although the blast furnace closed down probably in about 1755 – with production transferred to Newland – the forge continued to work until 1840, when the site was known as Nibthwaite Forge. A forge operated at Newland from 1783 until 1807, its short life probably due to the proximity of the sister site at Nibthwaite, just six miles away. A late-established forge at Lowwood was demolished in 1785. No forges were established at Duddon or Penny Bridge, which had access to off-site forges, in the case of Duddon in the Midlands.

Although some of the bar iron was sold locally, much went to Liverpool for use in the shipyards, while in the later 18th century some was used in the manufacture of boiler plates (Fell 1908, 253–4). The Furness ironmasters experimented with other products. Cast iron boilers, kettles and pans were made from 1721 onwards and by the 1740s more complex pieces, such as firegrates, were being cast. Iron ballast for the Royal Navy was cast at Backbarrow in 1739–40 and at Lowwood and Duddon in about 1755 (King 1995, 17–18). Cannon were cast at Backbarrow in 1742 and 1758 and at Nibthwaite in 1745; some of the Backbarrow guns failed in proving, however. On the other hand, shot was cast successfully at Newland, Leighton, Pennybridge, Backbarrow and the Argyll furnaces in the middle and later decades of the 18th century and shipped to Woolwich. A coal-fired anchor smithy was established at Backbarrow in 1753 and worked until 1773. The Argyll furnaces produced mainly pigs, which were shipped to Furness and elsewhere for forging. The Rawlinsons of the Backbarrow Company made use of their Quaker connections to establish trading links with Bristol, Lancaster, Warrington and Whitehaven. It is also noteworthy that the Furness iron companies diversified into timber and bark dealing (Marshall 1958, 21 and 24–5).

Raw materials and products were transported where possible by water, on Windermere and Coniston and on the lower reaches of the Duddon, Crake and Leven from specially constructed jetties; they were also shipped extensively around the western coasts of Britain. The construction of the Ulverston Canal, opened in 1796, and the Furness and Eskdale Railways, opened in 1846 and 1875 respectively, represent attempts – not altogether successful – to keep abreast of developments in transport.

Furness bar iron was of very high quality, but the introduction of the puddling process from the 1780s made cheaper iron available. Although this was inferior, it proved adequate for many purposes. From the late 19th century, the increasing availability of steel (which was also cheap relative to bar iron) for higher quality work put an end to the demand for bar iron. This, together with the application of steam power to iron processing and the inexorable rise of the

coke-based industry which tied ironworks to the coalfields rather than the woodlands, led to the ultimate demise of the charcoal-based industry in Furness. As seen above, the blast furnaces closed one after another from the 1750s, though three survived until the late 19th century and one, Backbarrow, into the 20th.

The establishment of the blast furnaces caused a massive rise in the demand for charcoal. Charcoal burners or 'colliers' were subsequently brought in from other parts of the country to work the woods of High Furness (Fig 1.6). The second half of the 18th century saw a peak in the number of charcoal burners. Numbers declined in the 19th century as the charcoal-based iron industry contracted; the bobbin mills and the gunpowder industry, which in part replaced the ironworks, stimulated the demand for coppice wood but not for the labour of the colliers – the gunpowder works made their charcoal on site in metal clamps, giving a product of more predictable quality. Charcoal burning is a seasonal occupation and the colliers were employed for the rest of the year peeling bark for the tanning industry, burning bracken and brashings to make potash for the soap industry, and in woodland management or agricultural tasks. The increasing use of new chemicals in these industries and bulk imports of poles and bark from America drove down the demand for these other woodland crafts. By the early 20th century, coppice management was being abandoned and the charcoal burners described by Arthur Ransome (for example 1930, chapter 13) were a relatively rare sight.

Figure 1.6 Charcoal burners building a stack on a pitstead, showing huts, screens, water barrels and sacks of charcoal from a previous burn (Alfred Heaton Cooper).

2
Raw Materials

Possible early iron ore extraction sites

With the exception of the old working with prehistoric implements near Stainton mentioned in the previous chapter, no definite early iron extraction sites in Furness or south-west Cumbria are known. Few will have survived, given the intensity of mining activity in the 18th, 19th and 20th centuries. Nevertheless, some possible traces of earlier mining activity can be noted.

In Eskdale, the documentary history for iron mining begins in 1845, but it is unlikely that the documents give the full picture; almost certainly the visible outcropping veins would have been worked earlier. At Nab Gill iron mine, Boot, among the massive 19th-century workings are narrow grooves, made by picking ore from veins which seem too slight to have been of commercial interest to the Victorian miners. On high ground at the north-west end of the mine are clear traces of surface mining which could be of almost any date, but some of the trenches have been partly overlain or destroyed by the 19th-century workings and must, therefore, be earlier. A path down the fellside may have been a packhorse track carrying ore from these workings (*see* Fig 2.5). In Low Furness there are at least two sites which may retain traces of early mining.

Urswick stone walls (Fig 2.1)

The prehistoric settlement of Urswick Stone Walls (SD 260 742) lies on the north side of a low hill formed from horizontal beds of Lower Carboniferous limestone. These outcrop as crags and extensive limestone pavement, forming a series of curving terraces. The site occupies fields now under permanent pasture (although there is evidence of medieval or early post-medieval cultivation) and an area of dense overgrown coppiced woodland.

It comprises two enclosures, the remains of a field system, traces of iron mining and also a reputed bloomery site.

The two enclosures are distinct from one another, one being an irregular oval (Fig 2.1, a) and the other sharply rectilinear (Fig 2.1, b) – almost square indeed – and while they may or may not be contemporary some overlap at least seems likely. The oval enclosure, which has an entrance to the south-east and is sub-divided by internal walls, contains a central stone-built roundhouse and four possible subsidiary buildings. It was extensively excavated in 1906 (Dobson 1907) and dated to the Iron Age or Romano-British period by the finds – pieces of quernstone, a small fragment of decorated bronze sheet and some pottery sherds. Other finds included a flint scraper, animal bones and numerous fragments of hematite. The square enclosure has been badly damaged by quarrying. There are two entrances in the south-east side. One may be original but the other is almost certainly a later breach for quarry access. No internal features can be seen. The field system, which may be contemporary with the enclosures, consists of a series of boulder walls defining small irregular fields.

An ore vein runs along the south side of the enclosures. Along the line of the vein, the soil in a band about 10m wide shows intense red staining. This deposit was exploited by a shaft mine (Fig 2.1, c) which operated some time between 1846 and 1889, and of which the spoilheap, the engine house, the shaft head and a magazine – located 100m away – can be identified. The vein had also, however, previously been exploited by surface quarrying. The ore seems to have been extracted in a series of open workings (Fig 2.1, d–d) which survive to a depth of up to 1.6m; in one place exposed bedrock shows that the vein was only 0.7m thick. These excavations are separated from each other by unmined

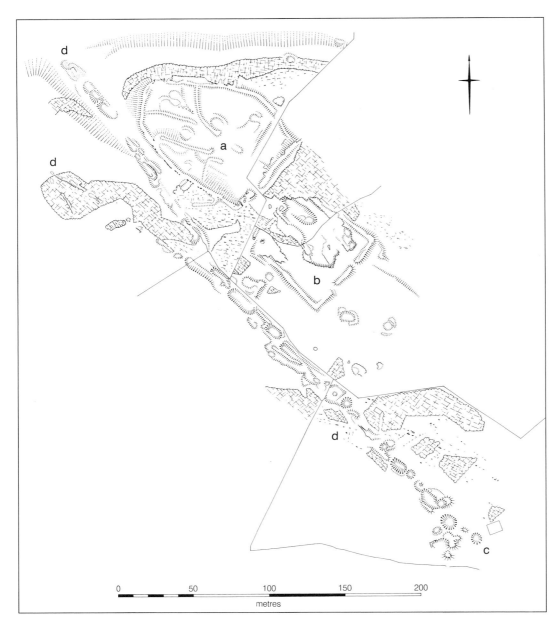

Figure 2.1 Urswick Stone Walls.

sections 1m–15m in length. Spoil has been dumped on either side of the excavations in heaps up to 1m high. The workings continue to the north-east where the vein splits and the workings follow parallel courses some 7m apart before one vein veers away to the west. The workings on this western vein are up to 2.1m deep and the width of the vein varies between 0.5 and 2.0m. Where the workings extend out of the woodland into pasture they have been backfilled.

It is clear from the earliest surviving antiquarian description of the site, by Thomas West in 1805, that these surface workings predate that time and were not

then within living memory. Given their proximity to the prehistoric settlement, their unsophisticated appearance and the finds of hematite within the enclosure, it is tempting to suggest that these workings might be contemporary with the settlement. Proximity cannot be taken to indicate contemporaneity, however, an unsophisticated appearance is not necessarily an indication of early date and the finds of hematite in the enclosure, which had been substantially disturbed prior to the excavation, were not stratified. Furthermore, open working to trace the course and strength of veins is known to have occurred in the 18th and 19th centuries. For all these reasons, an early date for these workings cannot be assumed. The question of their date therefore remains open – even further archaeological excavation may be unable to resolve it. Corroborative evidence, in the form of a nearby early smelting site, for instance, would be helpful.

Fell noted the existence of a bloomery at Urswick Stone Walls (1908, 171) but his siting is imprecise; Dobson claimed to have identified the site near the square enclosure, but his description of it as 'revealed by the damp colour of the soil turned up by moles' (1909, 137–42) does not carry conviction, and no trace of slag was found in the course of RCHME fieldwork. There is no sign of a bloomery at the site indicated by Dobson but the site identified by Fell may yet remain to be discovered.

Bolton Heads

About 1km to the south-west of Urswick Stone Walls lies Bolton Heads (SD 255 733), an area of open permanent pasture with some exposures of limestone pavement sloping gently from west to east. A rectilinear enclosure, not unlike that at Urswick Stone Walls, occupies a prominent position at the top of the slope at about 75m OD. To the north of this enclosure at least two north-west trending iron ore veins have been worked by surface digging in a manner very similar to that described above at Urswick Stone Walls.

It is known that unsuccessful trials for ore were made at Bolton Heads between 1750 and 1756 (Fell 1908, 64); on aerial photographs (for example Fig 2.2) it appears that some of the workings are cutting through ridge-and-furrow and presumably date to this episode. Whether the remains of surface extraction now visible are all attributable to this phase of activity, however, or whether some of them result from earlier mining is not certain. Again the question remains open, for the present at least.

Iron ore mines

The iron ore deposits of Cumbria lie in three main concentrations down the west coast, behind Whitehaven, in Eskdale and in Low Furness, with a few outliers in the high fells of the interior, for example at Langdale and Coniston. The charcoal-based industry of Furness was supplied mainly from its own orefield and that in Eskdale, although ore from Langdale and Coniston was recorded at Hacket forge in 1709 (Fell 1908, 198), and was probably used at Coniston forge as well.

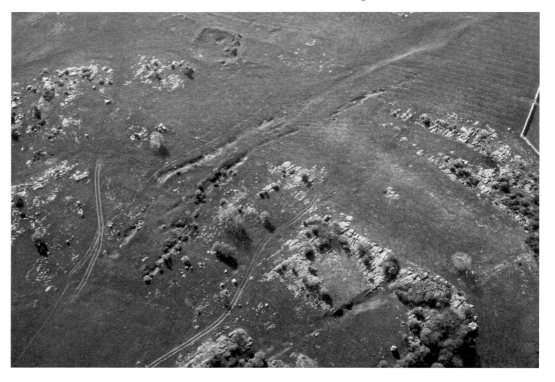

Figure 2.2 Bolton Heads: the square enclosure is top centre with the worked veins running from the top right corner. Ridge-and-furrow cultivation is visible between the areas of limestone pavement (NMR 12980/32).

While the mines in Eskdale, with the exception of Nab Gill, were small and have made relatively little impact on the landscape, those in Low Furness became massive undertakings with an effect that has been little short of devastating. The huge water-filled craters alongside the Duddon estuary are due to the extraction of the irregular masses, or 'sops', of ore which typify this area (Fig 2.3), whereas further to the south-east the ore tends to be in mineral vein form, leading to different patterns of exploitation.

In the medieval period, and probably before, most extraction was by surface working, as in the recorded 13th-century workings around the Dalton area. Deep mining had, however, commenced before the end of the 14th century. After the Dissolution, Furness Abbey's estates remained in Crown hands until 1613–14 when they were conveyed to private individuals. Even though very few mining leases appear to have been granted either by the Crown or its successors, the establishment of the blast furnaces from 1711 onwards created demand and the number of leases increased dramatically, especially in the late 1740s. In the 17th century and before, mining rights were severely restricted by the piecemeal pattern of land ownership, but by the mid-19th century, the orefields had been apportioned into mining royalties, most of which were leased by the furnace companies. The mines reached their peak of output in the 1880s (Fig 2.4). Decline thereafter was brought about by the exhaustion of deposits and by imports of cheaper ore. In Furness the last deep mine, Woodbine Pit, closed in 1946 and the last drift, Margaret Mine, Lindal, in 1960. On the other side of the Duddon, Hodbarrow Mine closed in 1968 (Hewer and McFadzean 1992, 89–90).

Mining methods were dictated largely by the form of the deposits. Where the ore was deposited in veins, the traditional method of 'stoping' was used. The vein would be cut from a shaft or adit in a series of steps, or stopes, above or below a haulage level, with waste, or 'deads', stored in previously mined voids; where the stopes were below the level, ore was raised in buckets called 'kibbles'. Where they were above the level, the miners could stand on the deads and drop the ore down chutes. In the more massive orebodies 'top-slicing' was the preferred method. This was similar to pillar-and-stall working in

coal mines except that here the pillars were also removed, allowing the roof to collapse onto the floor while another slice was being worked below. This required large amounts of timber for propping the working drifts, causing shortages in the 1780s which had to be supplied by imports from as far away as Norway (Fell 1908, 82). Wherever possible, therefore, pillars were left in place over several slices, leading to the creation of large chambers. The ore in the pillars was recovered after the chambers had collapsed. The workings were inherently unstable and when engine shafts were introduced in the 19th century, they had to be sunk through the adjacent country rock (Hewer and McFadzean 1992, 90).

Figure 2.3 (top) Subsidence at Park Mines, Askam, in the 1930s. At this time the water level was being controlled by an electric pump (Frank Woodall).

Figure 2.4 (above) Kathleen Pit, Roanhead Iron Mines: the engine house from the south c 1938 (Frank Woodall).

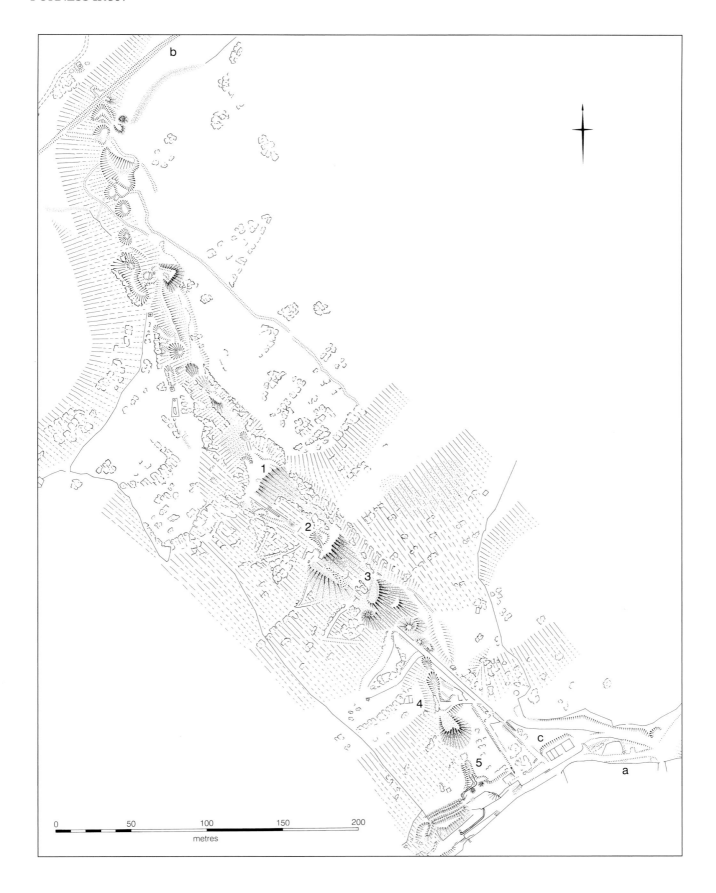

Miners were paid by the ton of ore won – the tribute system – and therefore had little commitment to the overall management and maintenance of the mine, leading to honeycomb workings and uncontrolled collapses (ibid, 105).

Ore was moved underground in wheelbarrows and tubs and raised to the surface in kibbles by horse-powered gins; steam winding engines were not introduced to the Furness mines until late in the 19th century. On the surface, the mining companies invested much time and labour in road building and improvements during the 18th century, although generally ore was taken to the nearest convenient point on the shore for loading onto small vessels. In the 19th century, tramways and mineral railways proliferated throughout the orefield.

Water was a constant hazard, but surprisingly steam pumping engines were not introduced until 1840, when, according to Fell (1908, 76), Cornish engines were installed at many pits. In the late 19th century, Cornish miners migrated to Furness as well.

In the following section specific relict landscapes are used to exemplify the various surface remains that survive and to illustrate something of the development and organisation of the later ore mines.

The Eskdale mines

Veins of hematite were worked at several places in Eskdale, which was part of the West Cumberland orefield, from at least the middle of the 19th century. Each mining complex comprises a series of adits ranging up the fellside, driving into vertical or near-vertical veins and opening onto flat-topped spoilheaps. The success of each mine is reflected, to some extent at least, by the size of these spoilheaps; at Blea Tarn (NY 167 007) and Gate Crag (SD 180 999), for instance, the adits are little more than prospecting trenches with very small amounts of spoil, while at the opposite extreme is Nab Gill, Boot (NY 173 013), with its massive heaps of waste, and inclined planes constructed to carry the ore down to the valley below.

Documentary evidence for mining in Eskdale, which has been summarised by Adams (1988, 117–24) and Kelly (1994, 115), begins in 1845 when S and J Lindow took a lease on Ban Garth (NY 153 008) and Nab Gill. They withdrew from the venture in 1856, however, and were succeeded by J Fearon who worked Ban Garth until the late 1860s. In 1871 the apparently mis-named Faithful Cookson sub-let the mines to Whitehaven Iron Mines Ltd, who drove a new level at Ban Garth and started the Blea Tarn mine. Their efforts were soon centred on Nab Gill, however, where the problem of the costs of carting the ore down the valley by road led, in 1872, to a bill in Parliament promoting the construction of a railway from Boot to Ravenglass (Davies 1968). The line was opened in 1875, but declining ore prices forced the company into liquidation in 1883, after raising 50,000 (imperial) tons of ore. Several subsequent attempts were made to re-open the mine but all failed, the last being in 1917. Mecklin Park mine (NY 129 020) opened in 1872, and the mines to the north of Christcliff (NY 185 011) and the Gill Force and Gate Crag mines were worked from 1880 until 1884 by the South Cumberland Iron Co. A branch line of the Eskdale Railway was opened to the Gill Force and Gate Crag mines without Parliamentary permission.

Nab Gill (Fig 2.5)

The Nab Gill mine was by far the most productive of the Eskdale mines and the remains of its surface workings are by far the most extensive. It takes its name from a distinct cleft on the line of the hematite vein near the top of the fellside to the north-west of the village of Boot. The workings extend from Whillan Beck up the boulder-strewn fellside to the shoulder of the dale, a height difference of about 150m, and onto the plateau above. On the plateau are large areas of subsidence into underground workings, some small surface workings or prospecting trenches and the heads of two ventilation shafts. Massive spoilheaps spread down the fellside alongside the remains of three inclined planes and a track system. At the bottom are the ruins of the mine offices situated on a loading platform above the turf-covered remains of Boot railway station and sidings.

There were five adits and two additional internal levels, all interconnected within the mine. Adit 1 was over 400m long. It has been possible to relate the underground workings, shown in a section of 1881 (published by Adams 1988, 120–1), to the surface remains with confidence, and to

Figure 2.5 (facing page) Nab Gill Mine, Boot, Eskdale.

verify on the ground the positions of the five adit portals (numbered 1 to 5 in descending order) and two of the three ventilation shafts. The section suggests that the vein pinched out to the north-west but also that the higher levels were more productive. This is reflected in the greater size of the spoilheaps at the entrances of adits 1 to 3. A sixth adit (Fig 2.5, a) exists beside Whillan Beck close to the valley floor. Postlethwaite mentions six levels at Nab Gill (1913, 138) and this may account for this new discovery, which must post-date 1881. This may have been an unauthorised and unsuccessful venture that was never documented or it may have been the working of the 'bottom level' in 1909–12 and 1917 (Adams 1988, 123–4). All the adits are now blocked by subsidence or by waste material from workings above. The only visible structural remains are the approaches, up to 2m wide, lined by drystone walls. Each one opens onto a terrace of debris from which spoil was tipped. These formed fan-shaped heaps up to 30m high, from which ore was transported down the hill, initially by a track and – from the early 1870s – by inclined plane. Adit 4 is served by a track which overlies the inclined planes, however, showing that, whenever it was originally driven, it was re-opened after the demise of the inclines.

The OS 1st edition 6in map of 1860 depicts a track climbing the hill from Boot to an 'Iron Mine' that can be identified as adit 3; no other mines or tracks are shown. Much of this well engineered track remains, measuring 4m to 6m wide and revetted on the downhill side, where necessary, by a drystone retaining wall up to 1.4m high. It is overlain by the inclines and by spoil from adit 3, which was reworked in the 1870s. The inclined planes were built by Whitehaven Iron Mines Ltd to run from the highest level (adit 1) down to the loading platform above the railway. They are 2.7m–4m wide and retained by drystone walls up to 1.8m high. The longest runs from the loading platform to adit 2, a horizontal distance of about 210m. At the head of this incline are some low ruinous walls – the foundations of its engine and winch houses. Adits 1 and 4 were served by separate inclines. A path, 1m wide and revetted on the downhill side where necessary, climbs the fellside from adit 3 to adit 1 and then on to the plateau; it avoids the line of the incline, suggesting that they may be contemporary, the path being simply foot access to the upper workings for the miners. Alternatively, it may have been a packhorse track by which ore was carried down the valley side from the surface workings above Nab Gill which, as noted above, may predate 1845.

Substantial collapses, where stopes neared or reached the surface, show as deep depressions or as holes or gashes in which, here and there, stoping timbers can be seen. The course of the main vein can be traced on the plateau as a discontinuous line of such depressions, as well as by the small surface workings.

Prior to the mining, water would have flowed naturally down Nab Gill. At some time, probably soon after 1871, a substantial drain (Fig 2.5, b), up to 0.9m deep and 3m wide, was cut across the headwaters of the gill to the north-west of the workings to divert surface water away from the mines. This drain has subsequently been breached and water now flows into one of the subsidence hollows and re-emerges from adit 5.

The stone-built mine offices, smithy and store (Fig 2.5, c) by the station are now unroofed but the walls survive to gable height on the south-west. They were almost certainly built at the same time as the railway. The station buildings, which were of timber construction, have not survived. A number of other small ruinous buildings are scattered near the workings; their functions are uncertain and they are not all necessarily connected with the mines.

Of the other Eskdale mines only those at Ban Garth, Christcliff and Gill Force approach Nab Gill in size and complexity, with large spoilheaps, inclined planes and railheads.

Low Furness mines

As noted above, Low Furness is littered with the remains, in various forms, of iron mines. Many of these have been the subject of detailed recording and study by members of the Cumbria Amenity Trust Mining History Society (CATMHS). During the course of the RCHME project two sites were recorded in detail, at Urswick Stone Walls (described above) and at Stone Closes. These may be taken as reasonably typical of the later 19th-century mines.

Stone Closes (Fig 2.6)

At Stone Closes (SD 250 732) are the remains of two small-scale shaft mines, both dating to the second half of the 19th century. An ore vein forks beneath Stone Closes, with one branch diverging in a northerly direction; one of the main mineshafts apparently overlies this fork.

The name 'Stone Closes' originally described a broad ridge of limestone, outcropping in places, extending from the southern periphery of the mine workings down to the village of Stainton with Adgarley, some 0.7km to the south. Much of this limestone ridge has been removed by quarrying which continues to date (1998). The establishment of the Devonshire Quarry at the southern end of the ridge in about 1866 saw the start of intensive extraction; since then the edge of the quarry has gradually crept northwards. 'Stone Closes' has, therefore, come to refer to an increasingly restricted area: early documentary references cannot automatically be equated with the site under discussion, since they could allude to any of a number of former mines which existed in the larger area, many of which lay close to Stainton village. The documentary evidence nevertheless highlights the fact that the locality was an important source of hematite and was widely regarded as the richest ore source in the district (Fell 1908, 94). In 1724, the Backbarrow and Cunsey Companies were mining 'in Stone Close' and by the end of the 18th century it was claimed that 'the works in Stone Close and Adgarley are the most flourishing that have been known in Furness' (West 1805, 40). Ore from this area was carried to Beanwell, on the Leven estuary, for shipment (Fell 1908, 91). It seems almost certain, however, that during the second half of the 19th century the method of transporting ore locally underwent some change, with the opening of the Stainton mineral branch of the Furness railway in 1866 (Joy 1983, 126); it is even possible that the branchline may have been the catalyst for the establishment of these particular mines.

The earthworks cluster in two discrete groups, each representing a separate mining operation. Both groups consist of shafts and spoilheaps but the southern group also includes the remains of an engine house. A number of the shaft heads – undesirable features for any stock farm – have recently

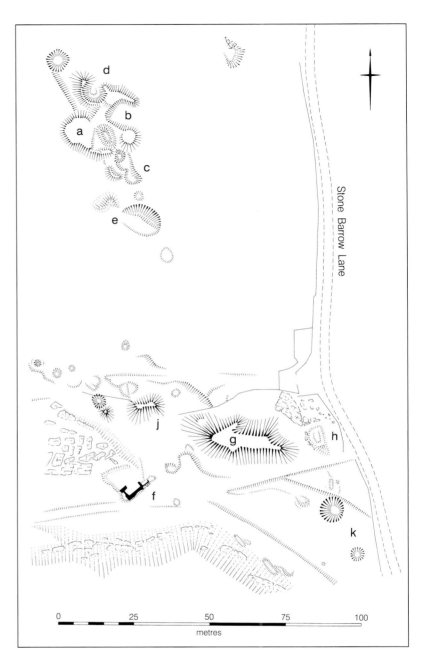

been backfilled with some of the spoil, a common occurrence threatening the survival of many similar mining sites in Low Furness.

The northern workings comprise five shafts accompanied by spoilheaps. Map evidence securely dates the working life of this mine to within a forty-year period, 1851–1890, although the small size of the earthworks implies that they were only operational for a short period within that time span. Central to this group, the main spoilheap (Fig 2.6, a) is composed of a pair

Figure 2.6 Stone Closes Mine, Stainton with Adgarley.

of contiguous flat-topped dumps, at the heart of which are the remains of a shaft head which has subsided, leaving a deep oval hollow. A curving limb of spoil extends in a north-easterly direction from the centre of the main spoilheap, partly enclosing a level area of ground (Fig 2.6, b), approximately 6.5m in diameter; it appears that the spoil has been dumped around something which was positioned at its centre, perhaps horse-powered winding gear.

Set into the south-eastern edge of this spoilheap is a much smaller shafthead, the surface remains being largely the result of subsidence. It overlies a broad uneven trench Fig 2.6, c), which is the earliest feature of the group stratigraphically, being overlain by the main spoilheap as well. This feature seems to be part of a prospecting trench dug to establish the best location for the shafts. A linear scarp which extends in a north-westerly direction from beneath the main spoilheap may be a continuation of this prospecting trench.

A large shafthead (Fig 2.6, d), on the northern side of the spoilheap, was – until recently – completely encircled by a high bank of earth, but a section of its bank on the northern side has been pushed into its centre. The shaft is marked on the OS 1:2 500 map of 1891 as a separate feature within the spoilheap and annotated 'old shaft'. Similarly, the largest mineshaft (Fig 2.6, e), situated at the south-eastern extremity of the group, has been partly backfilled by its adjacent spoilheap; both features are clearly shown on the 1891 map. At the north-western end of the group is a basin-shaped hollow which is unusual in having no associated spoil, suggesting that it may be the remains of a shaft which was infilled after abandonment but has subsequently settled; the practice of backfilling spent pits was customary and is documented as occurring at Stone Closes (Fell 1908, 83). The second, southern group of earthworks is focused upon the remains of the engine house, which would have held a steam pumping engine, and its associated mineshaft and spoilheap. The head of the mineshaft, which lay between the engine house and the spoilheap, had been completely infilled between 1994 and 1996, and its site is now marked by amorphous scarps.

Most of the engine house (Fig 2.6, f) is only visible as a broad depression cut into the natural slope and is now filled by dense-growing gorse bushes. On the south-eastern side of the structure, however, a wall of large limestone blocks up to 0.8m high is preserved. Within this wall are two vertical slots, 0.2m wide, recessed into the full height of the masonry, each accompanied by a smaller niche to one side; these are housings for machine fixings.

The engine house is depicted in some detail on the 1891 map but the physical remains and the cartographic evidence do not clearly correlate with one another. A circular structure depicted on the map midway along the north-eastern side of the building is, however, almost certainly the chimney. Its position suggests that the depression on the north-west side is the site of the boiler bay. The engine was still working in 1891 but no trace of it is shown on the revised map of 1913, indicating that the mine was abandoned during that period and that soon after abandonment it had come to resemble its present state. It is almost certain that after closure of the mine the plant would have been removed from the engine house and installed elsewhere; the building stone may have been removed for the same purpose or re-used locally.

The flat-topped spoilheap (Fig 2.6, g), which is 40m long, has two small finger dumps projecting from the main body of the tip. A displaced iron rail in the vicinity suggests that railed wagons were used to move the spoil. East of the spoilheap, sitting atop a small limestone outcrop, are the foundations of a small rectilinear building (Fig 2.6, h). The structure is shown on the 1891 map but disappears from later editions, indicating a short life; since it was contemporary with the engine house it is likely that it was associated with the mine.

At least two raised tracks, which could have carried wagonways, served the engine house. The first approaches from the south-east, following the bottom of the limestone ridge; it is defined by a single linear scarp, from which protrude the remains of a kerb of limestone blocks. The second track, also in the southern field, is oriented approximately east–west. Its course passes extremely close to the corner of the engine house, suggesting that the track may underlie the building; unfortunately the earthworks do not survive sufficiently well to clarify the matter.

A series of other small surface workings or shafts is situated to the north-west and to the south-east of the main shaft head, all following the same vein of ore. The spoil from these workings has been dumped against an angle in the former field wall creating a second, smaller spoilheap (Fig 2.6, j). In the south-east corner of the site are two further shaft heads (Fig 2.6, k) which have subsided to form cone-shaped hollows.

While it is certain that both mines are post-1850 and that the northernmost mine had ceased to operate before its neighbour, the cartographic evidence does not precisely answer the question of when each of the mines first opened. The contrast in the technology employed by the two sites for pumping during a short timespan may be significant. Steam engines were not commonly used in Furness iron mines until relatively late; even in the 1870s the industry had still not made the full transition from animal-powered pumping and winding gear and the region appears to have been regarded by contemporary writers as somewhat backward in this respect (Marshall 1958, 258). The more widespread adoption of steam pumping engines may have been at least partly driven by the desire to mine to greater depths at existing pits. This was because the search for new ore deposits was costly and could not guarantee success, making it desirable to exploit known deposits more fully. By about 1840, for example, a pumping engine was needed in order to obtain ore at Adgarley (Fell 1908, 64). It seems likely, therefore that (as might be expected) the less technologically sophisticated of the mines at Stone Close is the earlier of the two; the workings there may well suggest that greater returns would be available if mining at a greater depth could be achieved – it is tempting to see the smaller workings in the vicinity of the engine house as exploratory excavations to establish the best location for the new mine.

Fluxes

In a smelting furnace, the iron compounds/minerals in the ore are reduced to metallic iron that has to be separated from the unwanted material in the ore, known as 'gangue'. This is normally done by reacting the gangue to produce a slag which is liquid at the high temperatures within the furnace. This separates from the iron (which is solid in a bloomery furnace but liquid in a blast furnace) and can be 'tapped' out of the furnace. In a bloomery, some of the iron

was sacrificed to make an iron silicate slag but in a blast furnace, where the temperature was higher, a lime silicate slag, which had a higher melting point, could be produced. This was made by adding limestone to the charge. The limestone acts as a flux, reducing the operating temperature of the furnace and so reducing fuel consumption. The richness of the local hematite enabled the Furness ironmasters to use a lower ratio of limestone to ore in the furnace than elsewhere in the country, since the smaller percentage of gangue present in the ore required less flux (Schubert 1957, 232).

In Furness, fluxing was primarily a process used in the blast furnace and there is little documentary evidence relating to the use or procurement of limestone flux before the 18th century. The early bloomery furnaces would not have used flux but it is probable that those who worked the water-powered bloomforges, which were established from the mid-16th century, were familiar with the technique. In a description of a bloomforge at Milnthorpe on the River Beela (approximate site SD 49 81), written in 1675, it was stated explicitly that limestone flux was not used, with the implication that this was unusual. As Fell pointed out, 'it is probable that limestone was used as a flux at some forges for it was commonly known by the name of bloomery within recent years' (1908, 169–70 and 203–5).

Limestone quarries at Chapel Island, Ashes Wood and Roudsea Wood, all on the Leven estuary, supplied limestone to some of the blast furnaces (ibid, 231). These quarries are all situated on one of the main transport routes between the coast and High Furness. In Roudsea Wood the quarry is on the northern end of a long ridge of outcropping limestone (SD 331 827; see Fig 2.14, e). The larger but more distant deposits of limestone which straddle the Low Furness peninsula appear to have been exploited largely after the advent of the Furness Railway in the mid-19th century. The former Devonshire and Crown Quarries at Stainton, for example, provided flux for the steelworks at Hindpool (Farrer 1914, 329) via the Stainton mineral branch of the railway, which opened in 1866 (Joy 1983, 126). Once the rail network was established, the surviving charcoal-fired blast furnaces at Newland and Backbarrow may have received flux by rail.

Although limestone was most commonly used, alternative fluxing agents were employed. During the early 18th century, slag from bloomery sites was collected in large quantities. Bloomery slag not only contained significant amounts of iron, but may also have acted as a flux; it may not have been a very effective flux, in fact, but the ironmasters believed that it was. Most of this slag came from local bloomeries but it was also collected from the Forest of Dean (Fell 1908, 232). Even small quantities of bloomery slag appear to have been valued; a 'cynder heap' or bloomery mound in Turners Wood, 1km north of Backbarrow, was purchased by the company for £5 (ibid). The re-use of slag in this manner may have damaged or destroyed many bloomery sites. Pebbles of ironstone, called 'catspole' were collected from beaches around Ravenglass and Morecambe Bay and used in the same way as the bloomery slag. By about 1870 their use had been largely abandoned in favour of lithomarge, a compact china clay imported from Northern Ireland, and later fluorspar. All materials destined for the blast furnace needed to be kept dry but there were no dedicated stores used to house fluxes. The volume of flux would have been relatively small so it may have been kept with the ore; the partitioning of ore stores, as at Newland furnace, may be evidence of this.

Charcoal and related woodland industries

The existence of large tracts of broadleaved woodland across High Furness providing a reliable source of charcoal fuel was one of the determining factors in the establishment of an iron industry in the region. It was this important resource which allowed charcoal-fuelled ironmaking to flourish in Furness during the 18th and 19th centuries, at a time when much of the industry had converted to coke. The iron industry also stimulated demand for other wood and timber products, such as pit props and hammer beams. At the same time, the woods supplied the raw materials for a range of other industries including bark for tanning, potash for woollen cloth manufacture, wood for bobbin and brush stock manufacturing and charcoal for gunpowder production; during the 18th century arboriculture represented a highly profitable alternative to sheep farming in what was otherwise marginal land (Marshall and Davies-Shiel 1969, 166). The expansion of woodland onto former pasture land occurred at two of the woods investigated during the project and may be part of a wider response to the increased amounts of charcoal demanded by the blast furnaces. The woodlands are concentrated in the lake and river valleys of High Furness; they fringe the shores of Coniston Water and Lake Windermere and lie along the Grizedale Beck, Rusland valley, Crake valley and, further to the west, Dunnerdale. In the long term, industrial exploitation of this resource was not detrimental to the survival of woodland as a whole, although there is evidence to show that shortages of timber – as opposed to coppice wood – occurred quite frequently (Fell 1908, 106 and 125).

The commercial cultivation of deciduous woodland was reliant on coppicing, a traditional form of silviculture practised since prehistoric times. When felled, many species of tree do not die but produce new shoots from the stump or 'stool' which grow into straight poles in far greater numbers than occur naturally. When this 'underwood' is cut, the coppice stool will produce a second crop of shoots and the cycle will begin again; managing woods in this manner prolongs their productive life indefinitely. It was usual to grow some standard trees to maturity among the coppice wood in order to provide the large timbers needed for houses, ships and other substantial constructions. Standards might be self-seeded or allowed to mature from a 'singled' coppice stool and would have been cut after growing through a minimum of two coppice cycles (Jones 1993, 14). The length of time a coppice was allowed to grow before cutting varied between 14 and 25 years, although over 20 years was not common (Fell 1908, 132). To coppice large tracts of woodland successfully it was necessary to divide the woods into parcels which were at different stages in the rotation; these smaller parcels were called 'coupes', a name derived from the French verb couper, 'to cut' (Hendry *et al* 1984, 48). These divisions could be marked by streams, upright stones or most commonly by drystone walls. Coppiced wood was used to provide items such as barrel hoops, tool handles and bobbins as well as charcoal while the branches of the standards and any pollards – known as 'top and lop'– could be used for many purposes including charcoal, turned items, cartwheels and furniture. Nothing was wasted; even twigs were used to make besoms, or burnt to make potash. As well as providing excellent coppice poles, hazels produced a crop of nuts.

The woodland year

Woodland industries were seasonal, the optimum time for each activity being dictated by the growth cycle of trees. In the 19th century at least, the year began in October when wood sales took place. The standing crop was purchased at auction by a wood agent who usually agreed to remove the wood by a stipulated date or face a fine. He also hired the woodcutters, bark-peelers and charcoal burners (Jones 1993, 30; Satchell 1984, 94–5). The many small wood owners seem to have done their own charcoal burning, however, and the ironmasters frequently bought or leased woods.

Woodcutting began in about November and carried on until April, with the exception of the 'summerwood', or oak, which was reserved until spring when the rising sap made barking easier. Bark peeling took place throughout spring and early summer, almost certainly coinciding with the potash burning season. Lastly, charcoal burning occurred between August and early November. There is evidence to show that the divisions between the different occupations of the woodmen could be quite fluid; for example some woodcutters also worked as bark peelers or charcoal burners as well as husbandmen and labourers (Lambert 1991, 33).

Charcoal burning

Charcoal, which is composed mainly of carbon, is produced by the slow burning of wood in an oxygen-free atmosphere. As a fuel, it was preferred to wood because the absence of any moisture meant that it could produce temperatures of over 1000°C (Jones 1996, 67). The earliest accounts of charcoal burning or 'coaling' date to the 16th and 17th centuries. These demonstrate that, from this date at least, the process remained unchanged until it died out in the 1960s.

Charcoal was made within the woods on circular platforms known as 'pitsteads'.

A stake was driven into the centre of the pitstead around which upright lengths of cordwood were stacked concentrically to form a flattened dome. The stack was then sealed with a layer of bracken and turf covered by finely sieved soil or 'sammel' in order to keep out the air (Satchell 1984, 95). Wicker hurdles were placed around the stack to ensure that no uncontrolled draughts would allow the burn to get out of control. Finally the central stake was withdrawn, leaving an aperture which acted as a flue. Burning charcoal was tipped down the flue and when the stack was alight the hole was plugged with turf. During the burn, which might last up to two days, the stack had to be constantly watched and the seal of earth diligently maintained. The progress of the burn could be followed by watching the smoke, which changed from white to blue and finally ceased when the charcoal was ready. At that point, water was thrown on the mound, which was raked open, allowed to cool and the charcoal then bagged (Satchell 1984, 95).

The prime objective in making a pitstead was to create a level, stone-free area on which to construct the stack. The hilly terrain encountered in much of the woodland of High Furness has meant that the majority of pitsteads take the form of a circular or slightly oval platform terraced into the natural slope. The spoil created by digging into the ground to form the rear of the platform is pushed forward to make the front half. Sometimes the front and, less commonly, the back scarp of the pitstead is revetted by stone to give the structure more strength; in Heald Wood, on the western side of Windermere, the natural slope is especially steep, and the revetment of the front of all the pitsteads is unusually pronounced (Fig 2.7, right).

On more level ground, such measures were not necessary. Often all that remains is a slightly dished hollow enclosed by a low earthen bank, probably formed by the sweepings from the end of burn; good examples of this type may be seen at Stony Hazel (Fig 2.7, left). In some instances the earthworks are so slight that the eye is first drawn to a change in vegetation or the dark colour of the earth, stained black by charcoal dust. It was noted at most pitsteads that the ground was very dark and invariably contained fragments of charcoal, but only in minute traces and never at

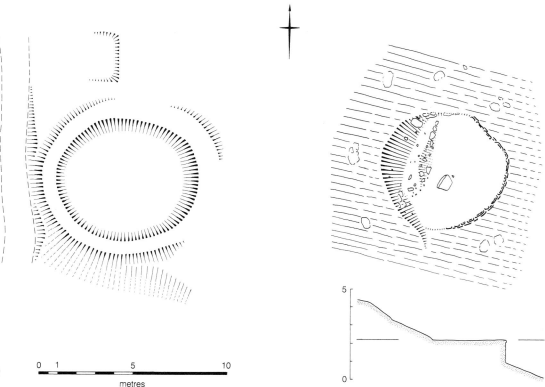

Figure 2.7
Comparative plans
of charcoal pitsteads
in Stony Hazel (left)
and Heald Wood.

0 1   5   10

metres

any distance from the pitstead; clearly there was little waste from a burn. In plan form, pitsteads usually survive as an oval rather than a circle due to slumping of the rear scarp over time but, allowing for this erosion, the average diameter is approximately 7.0m within a range of 5.5m to 8.0m. Small irregular hollows observed near many of the pitsteads may have been a source of 'sammel'.

Bark peeling

The bark of a number of species of tree, particularly oak, contains tannin which was the main active agent used to tan animal hides before the introduction of chemical substitutes in the 18th century. The processing of the bark occurred at the tanyard where it was ground up and put into vats of water for several weeks to form a tannin-rich solution in which pelts could be soaked. The demand for bark was such that it became a valuable commodity, sometimes fetching prices not very far below that of the underwood. Consequently, despite being a slow-growing tree, oak was coppiced in large numbers (Satchell 1984, 96; *see also* Howard-Davis 1987, 238).

The standards were stripped of as much of their bark as possible while standing, using a barking iron, firstly to score the outside and then to lever off pieces of bark from the trunk. The coppice poles were peeled after cutting, mounted on a long trestle at a suitable working height. The bark was left to dry, sometimes in heaps on the ground which might be protected from the rain by turves or thatching; if the bark got wet the tannin would leach away (Jones 1993, 52). Although some woods had dedicated bark barns (*see below*, Roudsea Wood, Haverthwaite; Fig 2.16), they were not common features and hay barns and cow houses were also used as temporary stores where available (Parsons 1997, 89). Bark peeling has left few visible traces.

Potash kilns

Potash is the common name for potassium hydroxide, which was produced by burning vegetation. It was used in the production of lye, an alkaline solution of potashes in water; traditionally, cloth was soaked in lye to remove impurities and wax as a preliminary to bleaching, although by the 19th century lye had been replaced by chemical agents (Cossons 1972, 16). The commercial production of potash, therefore, coincided with the expansion of the woollen industry during the 16th and 17th centuries and ended as chemical equivalents became widely available in the 19th century. Potash was made by burning greenery of different sorts – bracken, twigs, leaves and bark are all mentioned – in small kilns. A mid-19th-century description of potash making notes that the organic material was placed in a large iron pot – hence the name – which was inserted into the kiln, thereby making it easier to extract the ashes (Davies-Shiel 1973, 91). Earlier sources are less descriptive and do not make any mention of a cauldron; 16th-century sources refer to 'elying of asshes' and 'ealing hearths' rather than potashes, which may suggest that the introduction of a container for the ashes and perhaps a more robustly designed kiln to hold such a pot was a later development (Davies-Shiel 1973, 102; Fell 1908, 105–6).

Although large and sturdily constructed examples of potash kilns survive in the region, those kilns encountered during survey tended to be relatively small and simple stone-built structures (Fig 2.8, a and *see below*, Fig 2.13). Typically the kilns are circular and built into or against a natural slope allowing a flue to be incorporated into the front of the structure, opening at ground level.

Woodmens' huts

Some of the men employed in the woods were itinerant workers from beyond the Furness area but the majority were local (Lambert 1991, 33). Despite this, many woodmen needed to live in the woods where they worked because the lengthy coppice rotations necessitated moving to new woods each year. These might not always be situated conveniently enough for daily travel. In the summer months the wood-men's families sometimes joined them,

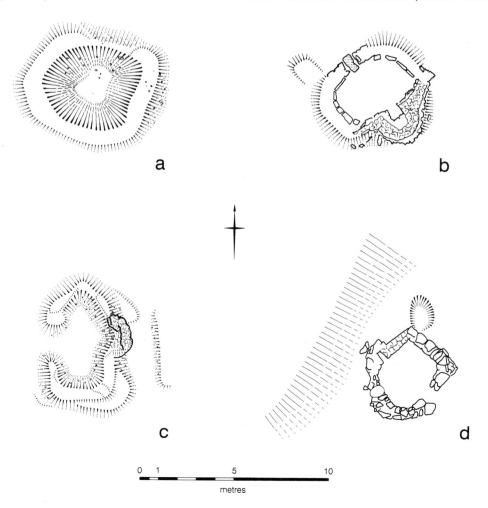

a

b

c

d

0 1   5   10

metres

Figure 2.8 Plan of a potash kiln in Roudsea Wood (a) and comparative plans of bark-peelers' huts in Roudsea Wood and Stony Hazel (b–d).

Figure 2.9 Interior of a charcoal-burners' hut at Bouth, near Haverthwaite, November 1908; the door faces onto the pitstead so that the stack can be kept under observation throughout the burn (Alfred Heaton Cooper).

Figure 2.10 (facing page) Bailiff Wood, High Barn Woods and Fair Hall Coppice, Coniston Water (for key see Fig 2.12)

all living together in temporary huts in the woods. Wives and older children were able to provide a supplementary income by making besoms and woven baskets known as 'swills', as well as helping with other chores. The woodmen's accommodation while they lived in the woods were temporary or semi-permanent huts, built largely of coppice poles and turves. The two distinct types of hut have come to be known as the bark-peelers' hut and the charcoal-burners' hut, the former being the more substantial of the two, with its stone chimney and low side walls of either turf or stone.

The plan shape of the bark-peelers' huts varies considerably; some are rectangular, others D shaped and some almost circular, but their size is fairly constant, averaging 3.7m × 2.7m internally (Fig 2.8, b–d). The side walls may be of stone or earth, the

latter originally being composed of turves supported by small panels of hurdling. The most prominent feature of all bark-peelers' huts is a stone-built chimney with a corbelled flue. The overall shape of the chimney is best observed in the turf-walled huts where the structure can be seen in isolation from the walls. They are semi-circular in plan, the back being rounded in the horizontal and vertical planes. In those huts which are entirely stone-built, the chimney may be subsumed into the general structure of the wall, protruding in a less visible manner. A common feature around the chimney, and to a lesser extent around the whole of the hut is a slight ditch, evidently to provide drainage and ensure that the interior of the hut (and the hearth in particular) remained dry. The single doorway is usually, but not exclusively, in the wall opposite the hearth. A substantial number of contemporary photographs, drawings and descriptions of huts survive, providing details of the perishable elements of the structure (for example Cowper 1901; Armstrong 1978). The framework for the roof was provided by four coppice poles sometimes lashed to a fifth ridge pole. Smaller poles rested on top of the surrounding side wall and were interwoven with laths to support a turfed roof held in place by the weight of further poles placed on top. The 'igloo' described by Arthur Ransome (1933, chapter 4) was a bark-peelers' hut.

In a significant number of cases the hearth is the only physical remnant of the hut; in some instances this may be due to the non-survival of the dwarf wall, especially where it was originally of turf. It may be suspected, however, that in some cases the lack of a dwarf wall is an original feature and that the hut represented a hybrid between the bark-peelers' hut and the charcoal-burners' hut. Usually reached by well defined tracks, the huts tend to occupy flatter ground such as natural plateaux, although a few stand on man-made building platforms.

The charcoal-burners' hut is simpler than the bark-peelers' hut, without side walls or a stone-built hearth. It was formed from a cluster of three main poles and roofed with turf in the same manner as the bark-peelers' hut (Cowper 1901; Fig 2.9). The lack of hearth and side walls has meant that archaeologically they have usually left no surface trace. Around pitsteads there are occasionally what appear to be the remains

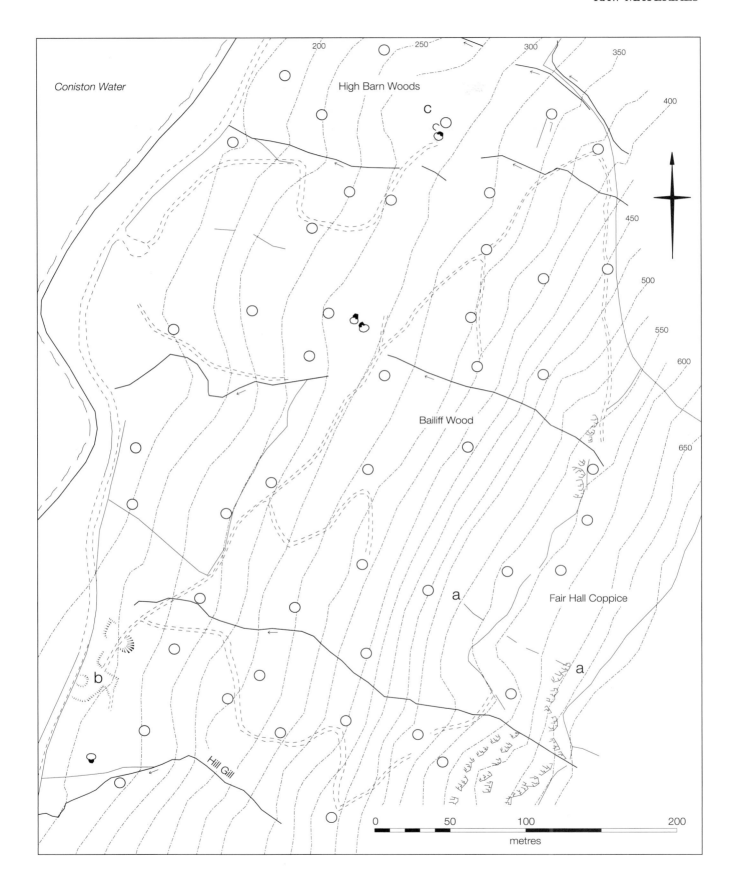

Coniston Water

High Barn Woods

c

Bailiff Wood

a

Fair Hall Coppice

a

b

Hill Gill

200
250
300
350
400
450
500
550
600
650

0   50   100   200

metres

of small platforms which might represent the sites of the huts. None of these is very well defined, however, and it is impossible to be certain that these features are not tree-throw holes. The floors of bark-peelers' huts are often sloping and no attempt has been made to create a level area, a feature which may be symptomatic of their status as temporary homes. The frequent absence of a specially created platform for the huts may explain why so few possible sites of charcoal-burners' huts have been detected. Bark-peelers' huts could be cleared out and re-used but the charcoal-burners' huts, having no permanent features, would have had a short life and over successive years their sites probably varied.

The lack of a hearth meant that cooking was usually done outside the charcoal-burners' hut but during wet weather a fire could be lit inside the hut and smoke allowed to filter through the door and roof turves (Lambert 1991, 33). Where colliers lived locally supplies of food were sometimes brought from their homes (Cowper 1901, 142).

Despite the overlap between the architectural styles of woodsmen's huts, the archaeological evidence recorded here supports the association of bark peeling and charcoal burning with different hut types. The distribution of bark-peelers' huts and pitsteads is quite different; some woods with many of the latter have few – if any – of the former and within any wood bark-peelers' huts are usually placed at some distance from the pitsteads; even where they do occur together, the huts face away from the pitsteads (*see below*, Fig 2.11), showing that they are not associated with charcoal burning.

Case studies

How these individual facets of woodland industry related to one another can be seen by looking at three woodland areas which were surveyed in detail.

Bailiff Wood, High Barn Woods and Fair Hall Coppice (Fig 2.10)

Along the eastern side of Coniston Water, the sharply rising valley side is covered by mature deciduous woodland for almost its entire length. Bailiff Wood, High Barn Woods and Fair Hall Coppice (SD 305 935), which together comprise 20ha, are representative of this area of woodland as a whole.

Oak is the predominant species with significant numbers of birch and hazel and some lime, holly and yew. A mix of standards and grown-out coppice can still be identified. The natural slope is steep but is broken by level terraces and low outcrops of rock.

The principal boundaries between the three woods can be identified, despite the fact that the walls are generally in a ruinous condition and only survive discontinuously. The walls, which were depicted on the OS map of 1851 in the same ruinous state in which they appear today, had clearly been allowed to deteriorate for some time. The reason for their neglect is uncertain but it might indicate that all three woods were managed as one by that date.

The configuration of the eastern boundary of Fair Hall Coppice is paralleled by the western, which may be an indication that this is a later intake of land. It contains four pitsteads which are laid out along its lower margin, one of them butting onto the pre-existing east wall of Bailiff Wood. The western boundary wall of Fair Hall Coppice is laid out at right angles to the fragmentary remains of another wall (Fig 2.10, a–a); their spatial relationship to one another suggests that the boundary of Fair Hall Coppice overlies the other, which may therefore be a remnant of a phase of enclosure pre-dating the woodland. It is interesting to note that Hill Gill almost certainly acted as the main boundary along the southern edge of Bailiff Wood. At the western end of Hill Gill, where the ground is less steep, a short length of wall, which runs from the roadside to a bend in the stream, marks the boundary in the conventional manner, but as the gradient increases the walling ceases, its course continued by the rushing gill. This raises the possibility that the other streams might have been used to demarcate coupes. Fragments of internal walling also survive; short sections of two separate walls in High Barn Woods may be evidence that it was originally divided into three smaller compartments, perhaps explaining the plural form of its name.

The pitsteads show an even distribution throughout all three woods; consequently many of the pitsteads are not situated close to a stream and the colliers must have had to collect water and store it in barrels nearby. Some of the pitsteads are clearly later than the walls, positioned so that the walls in effect provide revetment to the platforms. Over half of the pitsteads are served by tracks which traverse the slopes of the woods in a series of zig-zags. Most of these trackways join a principal track which runs diagonally through Bailiff Wood from south-west to north-east. One track hugs the exterior of High Barn Woods, an arrangement which emphasises the distinct points of access to Bailiff Wood and High Barn Woods and implies that the woods were originally under separate ownership. At the base of the main track, beside the road, is the site of a hogg-house or sheep shed (Fig 2.10, b) which could also have served as a temporary bark store. Its presence suggests that sheep were grazed within the woods at certain times of year or that the principal track served as a route to take stock up to summer grazing on the fells. It is even possible that the principal track originally skirted the former extent of the woodland, implying a third phase to the expansion of woodland.

There are five bark-peeler's huts. One of them (Fig 2.10, c and *see also* Fig 2.11) has turf walls and the remains of a stone hearth. It lies beside a dished pitstead but with its entrance facing away. The horse-shoe-shaped turf footings of what was apparently

a second hut lie to one side; it is unique in being the only such structure without a hearth discovered during the project and as such is the best example of what might be traditionally identified as a charcoal-burners' hut. An isolated hut in the south-west corner of Bailiff Wood contains much more stone in its walls than the other huts, suggesting that the nearby boundary wall was robbed for building material.

Parrock Wood, Rigg Wood and Knott End Wood (Fig 2.12)

These woods occupy the south-western end of Haverthwaite Heights (SD 343 845), the extreme south-western tip of a range of hills forming the watershed between the River Leven and Rusland Pool. The landform of the woods consists of two spurs diverging from a main plateau; Rigg Wood occupies the north-western spur, Knott End the precipitous tip of the southern spur and Parrock Wood takes in the rest of the area, including the upper reaches of the slight declivity between the two spurs. Most of Parrock Wood and part of Rigg Wood now consist of conifer plantations with occasional broadleaved trees. The 1888 OS map shows that at that time the woods contained a mix of deciduous and coniferous trees and that what is now an open field on the north-eastern edge of Knott End Wood was also wooded.

The most prominent feature archaeologically is the track dividing Rigg Wood from Parrock Wood, which follows the crest of the north-western spur and in places survives as a hollow-way. The track continues the alignment of a section of the former A590 below the woods and apparently at one time formed a crossroads beside the appropriately named Lane Ends Farm. The track is bounded on either side by a stone wall which becomes increasingly fragmentary and eventually disappears as it nears the cross roads. This suggests that its lower reaches have been robbed to provide material for Lane Ends Farm and its field walls. A second track runs through Rigg Wood along the base of the natural slope, linking the farm to fields beyond the woods and then swinging southwards to join the principal track. The latter part of the track is now a modern forestry route with no apparent indication of antiquity, but its relationship to other features, including another stretch of track crossing Parrock Wood, suggests that it may have had earlier origins. Other minor

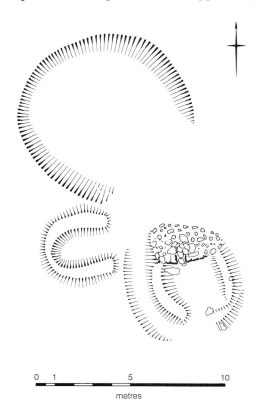

0 1   5   10

metres

Figure 2.11 Bailiff Wood: pitstead and huts at c on Figure 2.10.

Figure 2.12 Parrock Wood, Rigg Wood and Knott End Wood, Haverthwaite.

trackways, usually linking pitsteads or other features, are to be found within the woods but they are generally poorly defined and not as common as at either Bailiff or Roudsea Woods.

Rigg Wood was originally divided into two by a drystone wall, the footings of which can just be discerned. Fragments also survive of the boundary wall between Parrock and Knott End Woods, crossing the depression between the two spurs. Inside Parrock Wood are sections of two walls, which may have formed a smaller enclosure within it.

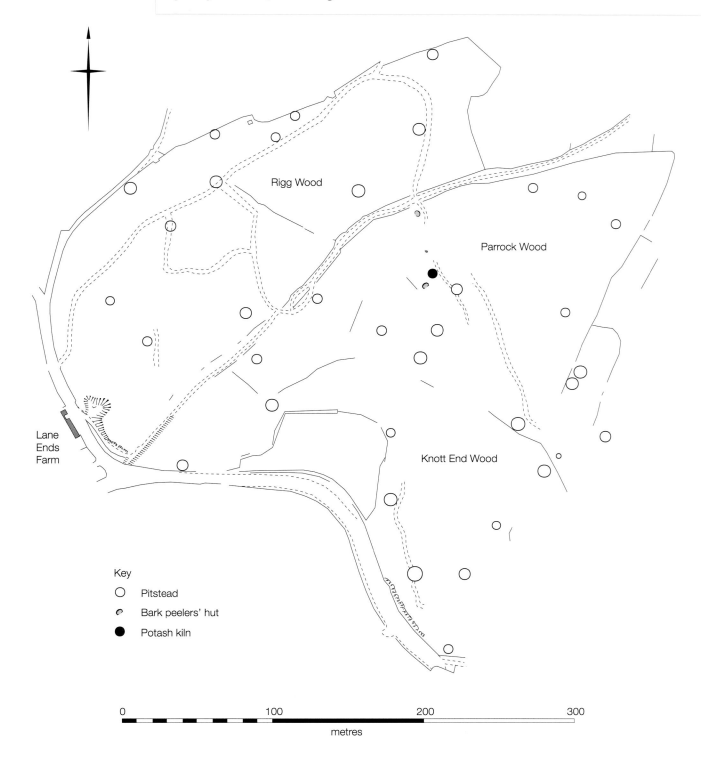

Rigg Wood

Parrock Wood

Lane
Ends
Farm

Knott End Wood

Key

○ Pitstead

◔ Bark peelers' hut

● Potash kiln

0   100   200   300

metres

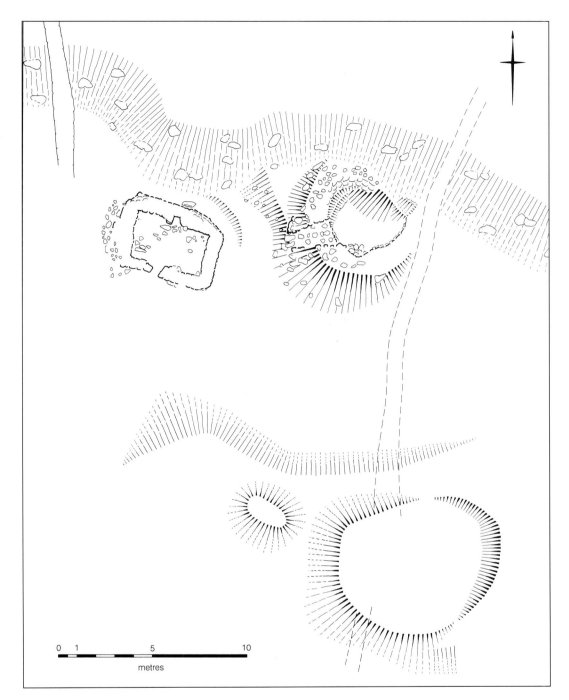

Figure 2.13 Parrock Wood: pitstead, hut and potash kiln.

0   1   5   10

metres

More intriguing are the two rectilinear fields adjoining the eastern edge of Parrock Wood, which appear to have been added on to an existing layout of enclosures. The walls bordering either side of the principal track splay out to create a funnel at its north-eastern end; this small triangle of land has later been enclosed by a wall containing the remains of a bee bole. The overall pattern of enclosure – and the presence of the bee bole – imply an agricultural phase pre-dating the woodland. Originally the main track passed through an enclosed landscape, which had evolved from the piecemeal creation of fields. Latterly the field boundaries may have acted as coppice divisions but it is clear from the decay of some of the walls that they decreased in importance.

Figure 2.14 (facing page) Roudsea Wood, near Haverthwaite.

The thirty-five known pitsteads are spread in a fairly even manner throughout the woods; any gaps in their distribution coincide with particularly steep or rocky areas of ground. There is a tendency for the pitsteads to be situated beside the walls, which provided ready made support for the platform. Very few exhibit evidence of stone revetment despite the fact that the majority are terraced into the natural slope. Occasionally the pitsteads are placed immediately downslope of a wall, possibly to gain shelter. Unusually, a pair of pitsteads occurs in one of the small enclosures on the eastern side of Parrock Wood.

There are two bark-peelers' huts, which lie only 40m apart. The northernmost is situated immediately adjacent to the principal track. The field wall beside the hut has been robbed to provide the material for the stone walls and hearth, emphasising that the importance of maintaining the field walls decreased as the land use changed. A second hut, to the south, forms part of a group of features (Fig 2.13), situated on a natural terrace, which also include a potash kiln and a pitstead. The bark-peeler's hut is also stone-built, rectangular, and with one of its long walls formed by a very flattened chimney.

Built into the bank of the terrace is a well preserved example of a potash kiln. Circular in plan, its interior consists of a deep pit whose outer wall has partly collapsed to form a broad earthen scarp. The site of the flue is represented by a lowering of the kiln wall to the south-west facing the rear of the hut, which might have been acting as a baffle against the prevailing wind. The stones used in the construction of the kiln and hut are almost certainly from a field wall, which is now reduced to its foundations, to the north-west of the terrace.

Roudsea Wood, Haverthwaite (Fig 2.14)
Roudsea Wood (SD 330 820) lies on the eastern bank of the River Leven, occupying a neck of land in a loop in the estuary. It encloses two parallel ridges of rock oriented NNW–SSE, which outcrop from the flood plain. The western ridge, of siltstones and mudstones, is covered by predominantly oak woodland while the eastern, limestone ridge supports ash, oak and lime. Pockets of marshy ground are common in the western half of the wood and substantial pooling of water, including Roudsea Tarn, occurs in

the declivity between the two ridges. Overall, the ground is undulating with rock outcrops but rarely steep. Roudsea is part of the Holker Estate but is now managed as a National Nature Reserve.

Of the numerous pitsteads within the wood none is revetted with stone because the ground is largely level; indeed, a number of charcoal-burning sites have no discernible earthworks and can be identified only by charcoal staining on the ground, usually accompanied by a slight change in vegetation and a lack of stones. These ephemeral remains suggest that in such low-lying woodland the locations of pitsteads changed more rapidly than in their more hilly counterparts.

Roudsea also possesses an unusually high number of both bark-peelers' huts and potash kilns – fourteen and ten respectively. In eight of the huts only the stone hearth survives; there is no indication of side walls, although half of those exhibit signs of a platform. The rest have side walls, mainly of earth but containing some stone, and vary in shape. An extremely well preserved example is situated near the centre of the wood (Fig 2.14, a; *see* Figs 2.8, b and 2.15). D shaped in plan, the stone chimney forms the south-eastern side of the hut. The hearth is directly opposite the entrance, which is paved by a single slate flagstone. The earth walls have been revetted along their internal face by upright slates. A second turf hut (Fig 2.8, c) displays an asymmetrical plan, one side being rectilinear, the other curved; it would be easy to attribute this shape to later damage but comparison with another, stone-built, example of this unusual form located in the woods around Stony Hazel (Fig 2.8, d) shows that this was probably its original design. Some of the pitsteads and huts utilise the shelter afforded by the low hollows between the ridges of outcropping rock. At the aptly named Windy Hills, on the western edge of the wood, a stone-built bark-peelers' hut occupies such a position and also has a stone baffle protecting the doorway.

The majority of the potash kilns are simple bowl-shaped hollows in the ground. At least half the kilns are dug into level ground, precluding the existence of a flue. An example of this type is found on the southern side of the wood (Fig 2.8, a) surrounded by a low bank of upcast soil. On the eastern side the bank is interrupted,

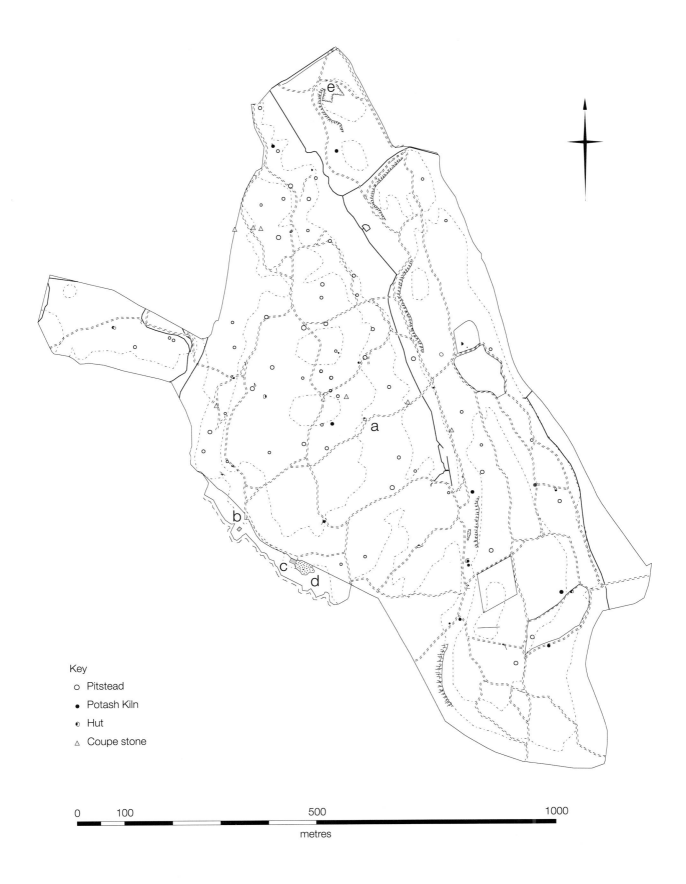

Key

o Pitstead

● Potash Kiln

◐ Hut

△ Coupe stone

0   100   500   1000

metres

*Figure 2.15
Roudsea: bark-
peelers' hut at a on
Fig 2.14, showing
partial reconstruction
of roof and
doorframe; see also
Fig 2.8, b (NMR
AA98/08248).*

suggesting that material was put in and removed at this point. The other kilns have been dug into natural scarps. The lowering at the front was probably the flue or raking-out hole. There is a single upstanding example, situated in a small quarry, whose walls spring from the quarried rock face.

The wood is bounded externally by a drystone wall but unusually the boundaries between the different coupes were marked not by walls but by 'coupe stones' – upright orthostats of slate, at least nine of which survive in a series of two or maybe three linear alignments. Since the stones cannot have acted as a physical boundary around the coupes, it can only be concluded that no grazing animals were permitted to wander through any part of the wood. At the end of the 19th century, the woods on the Holker estate were cut every sixteen years, a shorter rotation than other woods in the area (Lancashire Record Office, DDCa 18/203). A short section of drystone wall,

possibly with a return at one end, survives near the southern tip of the wood; this is the only evidence of an earlier boundary wall. A large network of paths traverses the wood, reflecting the relatively easy terrain compared to Bailiff and Parrock Woods. None of the pathways are coincident with the coupe boundaries, but the coupe stones commonly occur beside the trackways, suggesting that they were erected within an existing network of paths.

The main track leads north-south across the siltstone ridge to a former gunpowder magazine (Fig 2.14, b) beside the eastern shore of the estuary. The magazine stored gunpowder from the works at Lowwood, 1.5km to the north-east, prior to its transhipment by sea (Crocker 1988, 7). Not far from the magazine is a bark barn, a substantial stone building, rectangular in plan, one storey high and now roofless (Fig 2.16). Its front wall has been lost, and with it the evidence for doorways and other openings, but inside, vents in the base of the rear and end walls ensured that the underfloor area, divided by stone sleeper walls, was not damp. Above the floor, sawn-off timbers along much of the rear wall suggest an intermediate storage floor.

Immediately to the south-east of the bark barn is the site of a bloomery (Fig 2.14, d); tap slag and cinder cover an area approximately 28m in diameter but with no discernible earthworks or any identifiable centre. It appears that the slag heap has been at least partly disturbed by the construction of the bark barn which may overlie the edge of the bloomery. The paucity of the slag remains, despite their widespread distribution, may indicate that they were removed to one of the nearby blast furnaces to be resmelted. Although there are no visible remains of any jetty or wharf it seems likely that this estuarine site was used as a shipping point for a long period – firstly receiving ore and despatching iron, later transporting bark stored in the barn and finally gunpowder from the Lowwood works.

Figure 2.16
Roudsea: bark barn
(NMR
AA98/08243).

3

Processes

Transport

Most of the hematite deposits exploited to supply the Furness ironworks were concentrated in Low Furness, whereas the woodlands (which provided fuel) were in High Furness and its environs. The sheer volume of charcoal required to smelt the ore made it more economical to site the ironworks close to the fuel supplies and to transport the ore. One striking aspect of the transport system which evolved was the interplay between land-based and waterborne methods of transportation, the latter involving sea, rivers and lakes. Ore was taken by packhorse or cart from the mines to coastal wharves and then shipped to quays nearer the production sites. Windermere and Coniston Water and the rivers which issued from them – where navigable – provided parallel routes through this area for the movement of raw materials and products of many industries, notably iron, copper and slate. Further west, the Duddon Estuary operated in a similar manner.

The 18th-century blast furnaces at Cunsey, Backbarrow and Lowwood were served by a pair of quays situated 100m upstream from the highest normal tide level, on either side of the River Leven near Haverthwaite (Fig 3.1). The northern quay, a substantial structure built of stone (Fig 3.2), was known as Crane House and served Backbarrow and Cunsey. Crane House quay is in three sections, set at different angles. The central section is the most elaborate, its sloping face standing 1.3m high; it incorporates a flight of four steps, near which are the rusted stump of a mooring post and two grooves caused by mooring ropes wearing the upper edge of the quay. To the east, part of the original surface of massive flagstones survives. It received ore from coastal wharves on the north-western side of Morecambe Bay – Barrow End, Plumpton, Conishead Bank

and Beanwell – and from quays opposite Walney Island – Louzey Point and Palace Nook (Fell 1908, 39 and 425).

The southern quay, called Bigland Dock, survives as a stone-revetted platform; it probably served Lowwood. It is a much less substantial structure. A track, surviving as a terraceway, heads from the quay towards Lowwood. Around both quays the earth has been stained by the hematite which was shipped in and the presence of blast furnace slag on the riverbed suggests that this may have been shipped out as ballast.

The ore was taken from these two quays directly to Backbarrow and Lowwood, while that for Cunsey went by road to Newby Bridge, was reloaded into boats and rowed up Windermere to the furnace. Finished iron from Cunsey and Backbarrow was taken back along these routes to the sea (Fell 1908, 313). It seems likely that these supply routes developed before the 18th century, because all three blast furnaces are near the sites of earlier bloomforges established during the 17th century.

A similar communication pattern linked Morecambe Bay and Coniston Water. Ore shipped to quays at Penny Bridge and Greenodd, on the Leven Estuary, was taken by road to the blast furnace at Penny Bridge and further up the Crake valley to Nibthwaite furnace. Fell (1908, 221) refers to the construction of a quay at Pennybridge End in 1748 to serve the blast furnace then being built. The remains of this quay survive on the east bank of the Crake immediately below the old bridge; a section of the riverbank, 20m long, has been faced with coursed rubble walling and iron ore has stained the earth nearby. According to Collingwood (in Cowper 1898, 105), some of the iron ore used at the Tom Gill bloomeries, situated to the north of Coniston in Yewdale, was boated up the lake to a landing at its northern end.

Figure 3.1 (facing page) Quays on opposite banks of the Leven near Haverthwaite: they mark the south-western end of a well used inland route linking the coastal waters of the Furness peninsula with Windermere via Newby Bridge. They served the blast furnaces at Cunsey, Backbarrow and Lowwood.

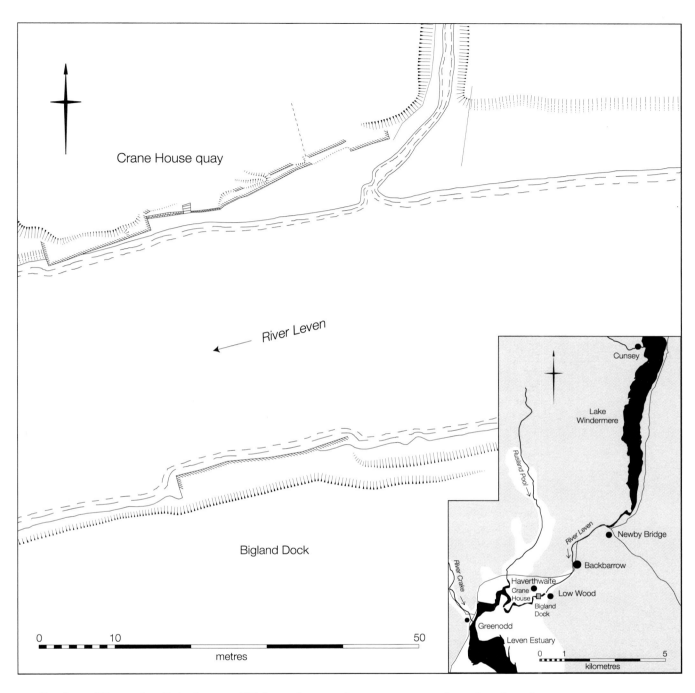

Crane House quay

River Leven

Bigland Dock

0   10   50

metres

Cunsey

Lake
Windermere

Rusland Pool

River Leven

Newby Bridge

Backbarrow

Haverthwaite
Crane
House   Low Wood

Bigland
Dock

River Crake

Greenodd

Leven Estuary

0   1   5

kilometres

Coniston Water also linked many High Furness bloomeries with the other major iron ore sources in the area, Langdale and Eskdale. Ore from Wetherlam and Langdale, for example, was transported to the bloomforge at Hacket (Collingwood 1925, 123). This source may also have supplied the large number of bloomeries, probably of pre-17th-century origin, which survive in the woods around Coniston Water (Collingwood 1902, 2). It is unlikely that much ore went southwards after the bloomforges were replaced by the blast furnaces, which relied heavily on ore from Low Furness. By 1713, pig iron produced at Backbarrow was being brought up Coniston Water via Nibthwaite quay and Waterhead to Hacket for refining (Fell 1908, 198). Nibthwaite quay, at the southern end of the lake, was also used by other local industries – slate, copper and gunpowder (Lowe 1968, 9). Its trade ceased

Figure 3.2
Crane House quay
(NMR AA98/03387).

following the construction of a railway line to Coniston, which took mineral traffic from 1860 (Norman 1994, 73). Although the quay has been considerably altered by the construction of a boathouse, it retains some historic features; areas of cobbles and paving are visible and the waterfront ends in a row of stone-built sheds erected for the storage of materials awaiting shipment (Lowe 1968, 8).

Ore for Duddon Furnace, where construction commenced in 1737, was transported overland from mines in Low Furness to Ireleth on the Duddon Estuary. From here it was shipped to wharves near Duddon Bridge and then taken by road to the ironworks (Morton 1962, 445). Marshall and Davies-Shiel publish a photograph of a quay below Duddon Bridge on the east bank of the river (1971, 83). The banks of the river below the bridge have now been revetted in stone, which appears to have destroyed or concealed the remains of any quays.

Shortages created by lack of labour – and commercial machinations – resulted in charcoal being brought in from further afield. During the 18th century, charcoal destined for Backbarrow and the other furnaces in the area was being brought down Windermere and Coniston Water by boat. Apparently, the boats were company-owned and were dragged between lakes as required to satisfy business demands. On Windermere, the charcoal sacks were loaded into vessels at Brathay and Bowness, rowed down the lake to landings at Newby Bridge and Townhead and transferred to land transport. Charcoal was also brought by sea. Around 1780 the Newland Company was buying woods in Scotland and erecting charcoal barns on the Galloway coast for storing charcoal prior to its shipment to Furness. In that year charcoal was brought from Scotland to provide extra fuel for both Newland and Nibthwaite (Fell 1908, 137–8).

Iron-rich bloomery slags were also brought to the smelting sites. Several hundred tons of slag were carted from Force Mill to Pennybridge Furnace. Some went to Backbarrow while the rest was shipped across Morecambe Bay for Leighton Furnace. Slag for the Backbarrow ironworks was also acquired from the Forest of Dean and shipped via Chepstow (ibid, 231–2).

In addition to supplying Furness, the hematite mines produced ore for ironworks elsewhere; this developed into a flourishing trade during the 18th century. Although most of the ore was shipped to South Wales, some went to Scotland and also to ironworks in the Leeds area via the North Sea and Hull. Shipping ore around the northern coasts was very expensive and was only feasible because vessels trading with the Baltic could be utilised (ibid, 325). While most of the iron produced in the 17th century was for local consumption (Phillips 1977a, 7), during the following century bar iron was being shipped to South Wales, Bristol, Liverpool and Ireland (Fell 1908, 253). Furness was also a major supplier of pig iron to forges in Staffordshire and Cheshire, the Black Country and Stour valley.

Before the construction of turnpike roads, overland routes in Furness were poor and in coastal parts involved hazardous crossings of the estuaries over the sands (Barnes 1968, 76–7). One surviving relic of these early overland routes is the Devil's Bridge (SD 2566 7959), a 17th- or 18th-century packhorse bridge at Horrace, on the road from Lindal Moor to Lowick Bridge. In order to facilitate the transport of ore, charcoal and iron, in some instances roads were widened, packhorse tracks converted into cart tracks and new roads built. The Newland Company, for example, built a road across the moss from Newland to the Plumpton Hall road in order to improve access between their ironworks and the wharves on the Leven Estuary

(Fell 1908, 303). The first turnpike trust in the area, set up in 1763, built a road between Kendal and Ireleth – the crossing point across the sands for Millom. This road linked a number of settlements connected with the iron industry, including Newby Bridge, Greenodd, Ulverston and Lindal. In 1819 another turnpike road was authorised, which ran northwards from Lancaster to join the Kendal-Ireleth turnpike at Greenodd via Carnforth, Milnthorpe, Newby Bridge, Backbarrow and Haverthwaite (Barnes 1968, 80).

During the second half of the 18th century, major changes to traditional transport patterns took place; the boating of ore and charcoal on the lakes, for instance, ceased following the closure of Cunsey Furnace (Fell 1908, 138). The opening of the Ulverston Canal in 1796 had major implications, especially for Newland Furnace, making its Plumpton landing redundant (John Marshall personal communication); the canal survives almost in its entirety. The shipping of ore to Crane House quay may also have come to an end during the early 19th century with the opening of the Kendal to Ireleth turnpike road.

In 1857, a railway line between Ulverston and Carnforth, built by the Ulverston and Lancaster Railway Company, superseded the Ulverston Canal. At Carnforth, this railway linked Furness to the rest of the country's expanding network of mainline railways (Barnes 1968, 90). The Furness Railway acquired the line in 1862. Their own line from Barrow had already reached Ulverston by 1854; one of the reasons for its construction was to transport ore from the mines around Dalton and Lindal to Barrow (Norman 1994, 7). Before the railways, mining companies had been forced to accumulate large stockpiles of ore at the coastal quays in order to compensate for those times of year when the roads from the mines were impassable. The railways overcame this problem by making transport possible at most times and facilitating efficient bulk movement – 600 to 700 (imperial) tons of ore could be transported along a railway line in a day (Marshall 1958, 196).

Towards the end of 1866, work commenced on a branch line from Plumpton Junction, on the Ulverston to Carnforth mainline, to Newby Bridge. It was extended to Lakeside in order to facilitate the

operation of larger steamers on Windermere and opened for passenger traffic in 1869 (Ballard 1974). The line provided a direct route between the iron ore mines and the Backbarrow ironworks, ending the dependency of the latter on water- and road-based transport. The ironworks were served by a short branch, which began at Haverthwaite station. It was laid out so that the wagons entered the ore store at high level and the ore could be discharged by gravity. The central and eastern parts of this branch have been removed but its route is still visible as a broad ledge. In the ore store, the beams which supported the track are also extant. In 1967 the railway closed to normal traffic but the section between Haverthwaite and Lakeside was re-opened in 1973 for passenger traffic (Ballard 1974; Norman 1994, 66–7). The transport of hematite from the upper end of Eskdale (at Boot) to the coast was also facilitated by the construction of a railway – in this case the three-foot gauge Ravenglass and Eskdale Railway, opened in 1875 (Davies 1968). The line closed in 1913 but two years later was re-opened to passengers, although the gauge was narrowed to 15in (381mm; Norman 1994, 53); it is still in use.

Bloomeries

Bloomeries are charcoal-fuelled iron smelting furnaces which produce wrought iron directly (in contrast to blast furnaces whose first product, cast iron, must be refined into wrought iron). The range of ironworking sites existing within this general class, based upon methods of power and numbers of hearths has been outlined above (Chapter 1: A note on terminology) but the technical and chemical processes are the same for all. During smelting the iron oxide in the ore is reduced leaving metallic iron, which forms a spongy mass or 'bloom' within the furnace. In addition, slag is produced from a combination of the gangue elements and some of the iron oxide; this liquates at over 1200°C, separating from the bloom and can be tapped off from the bottom of the furnace where it collects. Smelting in this manner is a 'batch process' and, though fuel and ore are added during the smelt, the size of the furnace limits the size of the resulting bloom. Once a smelt is complete the bloom is removed and must be hammered to squeeze out the residues of slag within it. This primary refining probably took place immediately to take advantage of the latent heat in the iron.

The difficulties of 'classifying' different categories of ironworking site have already been mentioned (Chapter 1: A note on terminology). In practice two types of bloomery were distinguished during archaeological survey: a simple bloomery, whose presence is usually marked solely by a mound of slag, and those much larger 'bloomforges' such as Muncaster Head, which are equipped with complex water management systems and may be accompanied by dedicated storage buildings. Of the former type of bloomery, only a handful have been excavated and none has provided dating evidence; little has changed in the 90 years since Fell wrote ' . . . these heaps of slag keep the secret of their age very closely. Not a coin, a piece of broken pottery, nor a relic of any kind has been found to tell their history' (1908, 168). Although bloomeries are mentioned in documents from the 12th century onwards, they have not been linked to known sites; in the absence of further evidence a medieval date is often assumed. It seems unlikely that a simple correlation exists between the size of a slag heap and the length of time a bloomery was in use. Many variables may have affected the rate of deposition, not least how regularly smelting occurred at any one site; to what extent the industry was seasonal – perhaps harmonised with charcoal burning – is an unknown factor.

Local place names, such as Cinder Hill, Cinderstone Beck and Black Beck are often clues to the presence of a bloomery. Some bloomery mounds are accompanied by remains of one or two stone buildings, which may be indicative of the permanence of such sites. Almost none exhibit conclusive evidence of having been water powered. A significant number of furnaces, while occurring in proximity to running water, were ill-situated to have made use of water power. This association must have been for other technical uses, such as puddling furnace clay and quenching, as well as for domestic use by the ironworkers. The furnaces of the simple bloomeries were probably cylindrical clay shafts, about 1–2m in height sitting atop a stone substructure. The furnace would have had a blowing hole to take the blast from the bellows and a small archway on one side to allow the slag to be tapped into a hollow outside. This type of furnace may also have been the norm in some of the early bloomforges although it has been suggested that latterly stone-built hearths with iron plates were used (Awty and Phillips 1980, 29). In contrast to the simple bloomeries, bloomforges are often well represented in documentary sources, which greatly enhances our understanding of such sites.

High Furness bloomeries

Though precise figures are not available and ratios will have varied, it is clear that several tons of charcoal were required to smelt one ton of ore in a bloomery. Given the much greater volume of charcoal per ton and its fragility, it is obviously more efficient to transport iron ore to the charcoal source for smelting. The bloomeries are, therefore, situated in the woods of High Furness. An additional factor is the possibility that deposits of bog ore, which is easier to smelt than hematite, may have been available for early small-scale smelting in the valleys of High Furness.

The sites surveyed are a representative sample, ranging from the simplest to the more complex, from a large and varied population (Davies-Shiel 1998) of well preserved sites with high archaeological potential. They have been identified primarily by their slag heaps, but display a range of other components, including buildings and water management systems. There is some slight evidence for the spatial organisation of sites (as at Colwith Wood) and technological development (Tom Gill).

Springs bloomery (Fig 3.3, a)
The bloomery at Springs (SD 302 954), on the western shore of Coniston Water, is one of a number of bloomeries found in similar locations up and down the lake. The turf-covered bloomery occupies the corner of an improved pasture field some 50m to the north-east of Hoathwaite Beck. Notable for its size, the oval mound measures a maximum of 35m × 20m, is up to 2m high and contains something in the order of 825–1100m^3 of material.

This bloomery was excavated in 1897 by WG Collingwood and HS Cowper who each published his own account (Cowper 1898; Collingwood 1902). They excavated a series of narrow trenches through the mound

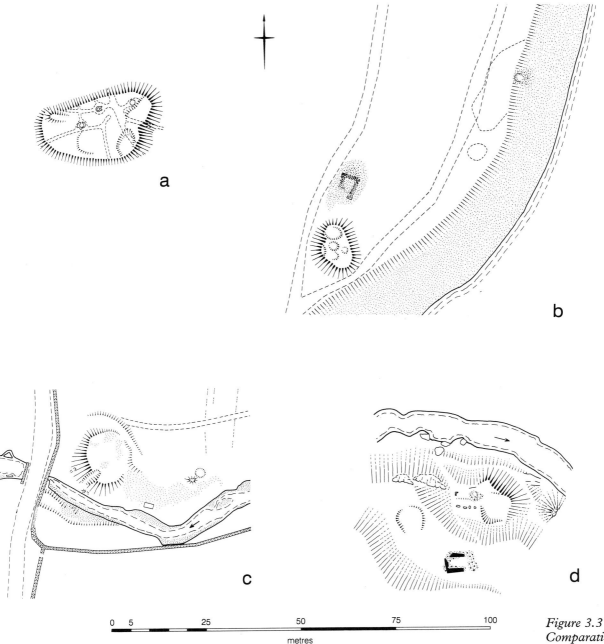

a

b

c

d

0 5   25   50   75   100

metres

Figure 3.3
Comparative plans
of High Furness
bloomeries: a Springs,
b Harrison Coppice,
c Beck Leven Foot
bloomery (the stone-
built rectangular
platform to the south-
east of the mound
was constructed by
T Clare during an
experimental smelting
exercise in the 1980s)
and d Colwith Force.

(pecked lines on Fig 3.3, a), which revealed variations in its composition below a top layer of earth. The south-eastern half was made up primarily of loose slag, although further deposits of slag to the south-west were more mixed with earth. In contrast, the northern quadrant of the mound was packed with charcoal. Most important was the discovery of three furnaces (indicated on Fig 3.3, a) and the site of a possible fourth. The best preserved example was described as a circular foundation of stones packed with clay, about 6ft 7in (2m) in diameter externally and up to 2ft 5in (0.7m) in height. A gap in the northern side of the furnace wall was identified as a blowing hole. Between two stub walls radiating from the exterior of the south-western side of the furnace was a small pit, which was thought to be the slag-tapping pit; this same arrangement was also observed at one of the other furnaces. Collingwood noticed that three of the furnaces had been covered over by slag, indicating successive rather than simultaneous use.

Harrison Coppice bloomery (Fig 3.3, b)
Two bloomery mounds, accompanied by the remains of a building, lie within Harrison Coppice (SD 299 943) on the western side of Coniston Water, only 1km south of Springs bloomery. This group of features occupies a low natural terrace above the shingle beach of the lakeside and is overlooked by rocky but densely wooded slopes.

The more upstanding of the two mounds, overgrown by trees and moss, is up to 1.1m high. A number of scoops and depressions pockmark its summit, revealing large quantities of slag and a number of unburnt stones. Beside the mound are the remains of a rectangular drystone building buried within its own debris. Few facing stones survive either *in situ* or displaced, suggesting that much of the good quality stone has been robbed. Although no facing is discernible in the interior, that which survives on the exterior demonstrates an overall size of about 6m × 4.8m. There is a concentration of tumbled stone at the northern end of the building, but at the southern end only a light scatter of stone, possibly marking the site of an entrance, which overlooks the bloomery mound. The evidence from geophysical survey at Colwith (see below) suggests the possibility that the furnace was inside the building.

The second slag heap (indicated by pecked lines on Fig 3.3, b) is little more than a slight swelling, not more than 0.15m high, situated on the edge of the terrace above the shore. Small pieces of bloomery slag are scattered around the mound among the forest litter. The precise extent of the bloomery mound is difficult to define because of the often vague edge of the visible slag but overall it measures approximately 26m × 10m. A small surface scatter of slag to the south of the mound should probably be regarded as part of the same feature, despite being physically separate.

Set into the edge of this low mound of slag, in the scarp which defines the edge of the terrace, is a potash kiln. Built of crude masonry, much of the kiln has collapsed onto the beach but a semicircle of stonework survives intact at the rear of the kiln, to a height of 1.5m, indicating an original diameter of about 2.4m. The potash kiln was noted by Collingwood and Cowper when they examined the site at the turn of the century and both misinterpreted the structure as the remains of a furnace (Cowper 1898, 91; Collingwood 1902, 14). Its position in relation to the slag appears to be fortuitous, however, and demonstrates that the potash burning post-dated the use of the bloomery.

Beck Leven Foot bloomery (Fig 3.3, c)
The bloomery mound at Beck Leven Foot (SD 301 952) is situated on the eastern side of Coniston Water about 70m from the lakeside. Surmounted by a small stand of trees, the bloomery lies in the corner of a pasture field, on the north bank of the beck. The mound, measuring some 19m × 15m overall, is over 1m high and is estimated to contain between 110–150m³ of material. There is much surface stone scattered around the site but there are no surviving structural remains associated with the bloomery.

The presence of a bloomery at this location has been noted by previous commentators (for example, Collingwood 1902; Fell 1908, 173) and more recently, *c* 1984, the mound was the subject of an excavation by T Clare. The remains of this excavation were still visible in 1996, comprising an open trench cut into the southern side of the mound and a spoilheap of slag, 0.8m high, beside the field wall on the western perimeter of the site; since then, the trench has been backfilled and the profile of the mound restored. The excavator found no trace of a furnace within the trench (which was not taken down as far as the ground surface), leading him to the conclusion that the mound was merely a waste tip and that the furnace or furnaces were situated outside it. If this is the case, Beck Leven may be viewed as an interesting contrast to Springs bloomery; however, given the percentage of the mound which remains uninvestigated, this assertion cannot be regarded as proven. Faint traces of broad ridge-and-furrow can be seen to the north of the bloomery, and geophysical survey suggests that this cultivation may have destroyed any structures connected with the bloomery in this area (P Crew personal communication).

Colwith Force bloomery (Fig 3.3, d)
Near the eastern end of Little Langdale is Colwith Force bloomery (NY 328 031) which lies on the southern bank of the River Brathay, 100m downstream from Colwith Force. Below the waterfall, the river has

carved out a deep channel with precipitous sides in places, notably on its northern bank, opposite the bloomery. The eastern half of Little Langdale is densely wooded and the site lies within an area of predominantly oak woodland known as Atkinson's Coppice. The archaeological remains, which comprise a slag heap and the foundations of two buildings, are situated on a pair of natural terraces, one above the other, overlooking the river.

The bloomery survives as a flat-topped dump of slag upon the lower terrace beside the river's edge. The exact size of the mound is difficult to gauge because the archaeological remains merge into the natural topography of the terrace. A small projection in the outline of the crest of the bloomery has the appearance of a small 'finger dump', suggesting that much of the waste was deliberately tipped from the terrace into the river; the northern scarp of the terrace is strewn with slag for some 21m of its length. Erosion of the river bank has exposed deposits of slag, charcoal and cinder, with a thickness of between 0.3m and 0.9m. The majority of slag is very heavy and often rusted indicating that it still contains a high proportion of iron.

A small stone building, approximately 5.5m × 4.5m externally, occupied the north-west corner of the lower terrace, but a few footing stones are all that survive of it. The foundation for the building appears to have been strengthened by revetment walling along the edge of the natural terrace. The topography dictates that the entrance must have been in the eastern wall, but it was not identifiable. This building appeared at first sight to be too confined to house a furnace and no slag was found in its interior. It is noticeable, nevertheless, that the finger dump of slag is immediately adjacent to the site of the entrance to the building, raising the possibility that slag was cleared from the interior and dumped to the side of the doorway. Further, geophysical survey has demonstrated the survival of two furnaces within this building (P Crew personal communication).

On the upper terrace, there are the remains of a second building. Although in a ruinous condition, the walls survive up to 0.7m high. There is an entrance in the south-eastern corner. Around the exterior of the eastern end of the building is a small scatter of hematite and the surrounding ground is stained pink; no traces of ore were discovered inside the building, but it may have been used to store the hematite. The bloomery is unlikely to have been taking ore from the Furness peninsula and was probably making use of nearer deposits in the Langdales, to the north-west of the Wrynose Pass, and perhaps as far west as Eskdale.

Despite the proximity of the river, the local topography appears to rule out the possibility that water power was used at the bloomery. The value of water for other purposes is illustrated by the presence of a revetted pathway to the north-east of the terrace, which leads directly to the water's edge. The river is neither navigable nor fordable at this point and the only conclusion is that the pathway was made to facilitate water collection from the river. The two terraces are joined by a trackway visible as a break of slope across the natural scarp. This trackway continues in a north-westerly direction past the rear of the building on the lower terrace and down to the river. An ill-defined track along the river's edge may have linked this track to the revetted pathway.

After the bloomery ceased to operate, the site was used for charcoal burning; the top of the bloomery mound is partly overlain by a pitstead whose crescentic backscarp has been cut to a depth of 0.8m. A second pitstead is situated on the upper terrace. The presence of the two buildings – assuming that they were habitable – may have made the site more attractive to charcoal burners.

Tom Gill bloomeries (Fig 3.4)

In Lane Head Coppice (SD 322 998), an area of oak woodland at the head of the glacial valley which contains Coniston Water, are the remains of two bloomeries, only 40m from one another. A stone-built channel in the side of Tom Gill may be the head of a former leat taking water to one of the bloomeries. A small slag mound (Fig 3.4, a) is situated on the northern bank of the gill, at the foot of a slope which is dominated by ridges of outcropping bedrock. As Tom Gill cascades over these ridges, it forms a series of small waterfalls; the stone channel is situated between two of these falls, above the bloomery mound. The general location of a second bloomery (3.4, b) is marked by a scatter of slag, distributed along the crest and slope of a high natural ravine overlooking the gill.

43

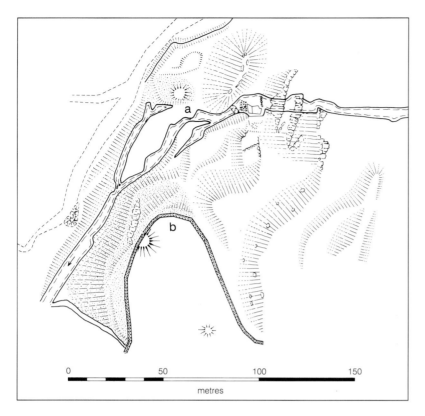

Figure 3.4
Tom Gill bloomeries.

partly cut into the bedrock, occupies part of a natural terrace adjacent to the bottom of a small waterfall about halfway up the series of falls described above. The level of the water in the pool at the foot of the waterfall appears to have been raised slightly by the construction of a simple stone dam or weir across the gill, but all that remains is a few large stones. The L-shaped channel is now filled with debris, but its original depth, 1.4m, is evident at its western end, which opens on to the top of another natural waterfall. The northern side of the channel is partly defined by the edge of a rectangular block of masonry, which probably served the additional purpose of revetting the edge of the stream to protect the channel when the gill was in spate. On the natural terrace are some slight scarps and possible stone footings, which may indicate the former existence of a more substantial structure.

The channel is of sufficient depth to have held a small undershot waterwheel, but the lack of slag in the vicinity of the channel argues against the possibility that smelting had taken place on the terrace beside the channel. An alternative explanation is that the channel is a short leat feeding a wooden launder to an overshot wheel powering bellows near the bloomery mound. A cursory examination of slag from the bloomery mound suggested that the furnaces had been run hotter than at other bloomery sites (P Crew and G McDonnell personal communication), which may also indicate the use of water power at this site.

The site of the second bloomery is indicated by the scatter of slag across the west-facing bluff above the gill; the furnace – or furnaces – must have sat on the flatter ground at the summit of the slope, in what is now part of an enclosed pasture field. Debris from the furnace may have been tipped into the gill after each smelting operation, so that the mound typical of such sites never accumulated. Alternatively, when the field was enclosed, the ground could have been cleared of any industrial waste, thereby creating the same effect but over a much shorter timespan. A slight mound, overlain by the field wall, showed no sign of slag but the earth, where exposed, was very dark. Geophysical survey confirms the presence of hearths in this area (P Crew personal communication).

The site, formerly known as Tarn Gill, was first recorded by H S Cowper (1898, 100), although it is apparent from his description that he had only observed the slag spread and was unaware of either the bloomery mound or the stone channel. A note at the end of Cowper's article states that 'Mr Collingwood says that the ore for . . . Tarn Gill [was landed] at the head of the lake near Mr. Marshall's boathouse; which accounts for the occasional pieces of slag and ore' (ibid, 105). Marshall's boathouse, although not named on the 1892 OS map, is probably the boathouse shown at SD 3159 9784. Collingwood's claim would appear to be based on speculation rather than fact, but it is true to say that the bloomeries at Tom Gill would have been well placed to take advantage of the traffic in ore along the lake.

The bloomery mound is small, measuring only 6.2m in diameter and 0.5m in height. It has been slightly eroded by the gill which runs past its southern edge, revealing black soil and small fragments of tap slag. Further slag is scattered across the ground nearby.

The stone channel is on the opposite side of the gill to the mound, and 20m upstream from it. This trough-like feature,

As Cowper argued (1898, 100), this bloomery does not appear to have been water powered. If it had been intended to use water power the bloomery could have been placed closer to Tom Gill; this crucial point may explain why two bloomeries exist in such close proximity to one another. The slag spread may represent the original bloomery site, at which the blast was provided by foot bellows. The centre of operations may subsequently have moved closer to the gill to enable water power to be adopted. Unfortunately, without independent dating, the development of the site as outlined here must remain conjectural since the three main elements of the site show no direct archaeological relationships with one another.

Muncaster Head bloomforge (Fig 3.5)

On 24 September 1636 William Wright of Brougham, ironmaster (Phillips 1977b), made an agreement with William Pennington to build a 'forge or ironworks' for the manufacture of bar iron on Pennington's land at Bank End by the River Esk, at what is now called Muncaster Head. All the timber and machinery for the forge, including hammer and anvil, three bloomery hearths with bellows and all necessary gear and tools were to be brought to the site ready to begin work by the end of the following September. There was also to be a dam or pond to control the water

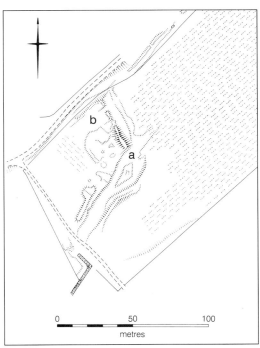

supply and ditches with flood gates to carry water to and from the forge. Pennington was to supply sufficient timber (oak was specified), gravel, clay sods, earth, stone and other materials to build the forge and make the dam, weir, ditches and races. Within a month of Wright completing the forge, Pennington was to supply 150 (imperial) tons of ore, while Wright would provide half the initial charcoal stock from his own woods. Wright was to set up a 'coal house' to store charcoal with timber supplied by Pennington, and Pennington was to allow the ironworkers the use of a dwelling house at Bank End for a term of five years. Wright and Pennington would be equal partners initially, but after 3,200 cords of wood had been used, the iron was to be divided one-third to Pennington and two-thirds to Wright (Cumbria Record Office, Carlisle, Pennington Papers D/P 185).

A bloomery site was identified at Muncaster Head (SD 1428 9891) in the 1920s. It was excavated in 1967–8, demonstrating beyond reasonable doubt that this was the bloomforge mentioned in the 17th-century document (Tylecote and Cherry 1970).

The excavations uncovered the wheelrace (Fig 3.5, a), 2m wide at the base, containing oak timbers which may have been the remains of an undershot wheel about 4.5m in diameter. The presence of this probable wheel, a short length of revetment wall and the remains of the by-pass channel to the south, suggested to the excavators the position of the forge hammer. The positions of the hearths and bellows were considered to be slightly upstream on the grounds that, with their smaller power requirements, the bellows could have been driven by wheels of lesser diameter placed higher in the race, but the excavation failed to locate them. A working floor composed of pebbles and sand was found, with charcoal spread over half of it. This floor had been covered by silt, presumably cleared out of the race, and a spread of slag. Among the charcoal on the floor were a number of pieces of clay tobacco pipes dating from c 1650 to c 1710. There was also a large heap of small fragments of charcoal, 10.5m in diameter and 0.5m high, representing about 5 (imperial) tons. Remains of a building were found to the south-west in an area heavily stained with hematite; initially this was

Figure 3.5 Muncaster Head bloomforge.

thought to have been the ore store but excavation apparently showed that it was a later building overlying the ore deposit. Another later agricultural building was found on top of the slag heap. As well as large quantities of charcoal and hematite (of local origin), the excavators found furnace bottoms, some tap slag, three pieces of cast iron, and pottery sherds dating from the early 17th to the early 18th century. The stone-built sluice gate on the leat 250m north-east of the bloomery was also excavated and found to be 1.2m high, with masonry slots on either side into which squared timbers could be inserted to regulate the water flow (Tylecote and Cherry 1970, 72–87).

The finding of cast iron objects on a bloomery site is interesting; if these pieces are of local origin they must post-date 1694 when the Cleator blast furnace was built, but it is of course possible that they were brought in from elsewhere. Two of the pieces are of 'white' iron – a hard, brittle iron formed by rapid cooling, suitable for conversion to malleable wrought iron (Wertime 1962, 16 and 19) – while the third contained nodular graphite, showing that it had been exposed to high temperatures since it was cast. Iron plates are known to have been used in bloomery, finery and chafery hearths, as at Milnthorpe in 1675 (Tylecote and Cherry 1970, 92–4). The slag was found to have a high phosphorus content, which the ore on site did not have. The phosphorus probably derived from the charcoal, which indicates that in this case the bark had probably not been peeled. Oak accounted for more than 70 per cent of the charcoal at Muncaster Head, with elm, ash, beech, birch, willow or poplar and hazel in small quantities (ibid, 96–8). From the weights of the furnace bottoms and the composition of the slag, the excavators calculated that the furnace yielded as much as 84 per cent of the iron content of the ore; this is extremely high for the period and could only have been obtained from a very high-grade ore, such as the local hematite (ibid, 103).

The site lies on the edge of the flood plain of the Esk and is currently under pasture, although the 330m-long leat from the river is partly within a conifer plantation. The remains, which are scant, have been severely affected by the excavations and, apparently, later ground disturbance. The site of the bloomery is bounded on the north-east by a large bank and on the south-east by the silted channels of the wheelrace and by-pass. The headrace leading to the works is silted, dry and incomplete, and the tailrace is lost, having apparently been replaced by the later field drainage pattern.

The site of the bloomery itself is reduced to an uneven terrace (Fig 3.5, b), up to 0.5m above the flood-plain, in which quantities of slag are exposed. The slight earthworks represent the pattern of the excavation trenches rather than the works themselves. The only structures still visible are parts of the two later agricultural buildings and traces of the wheelrace revetment. The race itself now forms a pond and is significantly wider than indicated on the excavators' plan. The most prominent feature is the bank bordering the north-east of the bloomery terrace. The purpose of this bank, which is up to 1.4m high, is uncertain. At its south-east end, slag and possible furnace bottoms protrude through the turf, while further to the north-west, it seems to consist of clean clay and pebbles. It is truncated by the present terraced track to Muncaster Head Farm. On the outer side of the bank is a shallow ditch, probably of relatively recent origin. The pond or dam mentioned in the 1636 document has not been located; if it was ever constructed it probably lay immediately to the north-east of the works where there is a slight depression. This area, like most of the field, is overlain by narrow ridge-and-furrow cultivation.

The excavation uncovered little structural evidence relevant to a bloomery forge and so the report dwells more upon speculative reconstruction of the original form of the works than upon the fine detail of the site. Some chance Romano-British finds on the site had led to suggestions that the bloomery was of Roman date, but the excavations found no evidence of Roman activity; the 17th-century date seems fairly established and the equation of the site with the forge documented in the 17th century can be accepted, although not absolutely proven. The existence of a water-powered facility is beyond doubt and the finding of slag and furnace bottoms indicates the presence of bloomery hearths. Firm evidence for the forge is lacking, however. Without the benefit of the documentary evidence, the site would probably be classified as a bloomery rather than a bloomforge.

Muncaster Head is the only bloomery or bloomforge site in Cumbria for which a secure archaeological date has so far been established. It is to be hoped that current and future research will provide not only a firm chronology for this important group of sites, but also a better understanding of them.

Blast furnaces

The change from the production of wrought iron by the bloomery process to that of cast iron in the blast furnace began in the south-east of England before 1500. By the end of the 17th century, the new technology had spread across much of Britain. In Cumbria, a few bloomforges continued in production into the early 18th century, but the principal development in Furness was the establishment of eight blast furnaces during the first half of the 18th century. All were charcoal fired and the industry was established because of the availability of high-quality hematite ore, water power and of extensive woods, which could be and were being coppiced for the production of charcoal. Details of how the iron was produced and the structure of blast furnaces are known from contemporary sources, notably a description of Leighton Furnace during the decade after its construction in 1711 (Ford and Fuller-Maitland 1931, 56–61), Diderot's *Encyclopaedia* (Gillespie 1959, *passim*) and Abraham Rees' *Cyclopedia* (Cossons 1972, **3**, 173–208), and from recent surveys (Crossley 1990, 153–85).

Processes

The production of pig iron in charcoal-fired blast furnaces involved smelting the charge of iron ore with the fuel and usually a limestone flux. Water-powered bellows raised the temperature sufficiently high to produce an alloy of iron and carbon, which could be run off from the base of the furnace in liquified form. During the 18th century, at least, ore was roasted to remove the dross. This and the other ingredients of the charge were added in particular proportions and in a certain order to prevent the mineral settling straight down through the centre and to stop it from crushing the charcoal. The good quality ore mined in Furness did not necessarily require much flux, although poorer quality

ore brought in from elsewhere may have needed more. During the smelting process, called a campaign, the molten iron trickled down through the furnace to settle in the hearth. Here the impurities floating on the top were drawn off as slag. Unless objects were being cast, the iron was drawn off through the tymp into a principal mould, the sow, with branches off known as pigs. The hard and brittle cast iron so formed, if not sold as such, was refined into malleable or wrought iron in a finery, either on the blast furnace site or away from it. Once a campaign was over and the furnace blown out, its interior was emptied and necessary repairs and relining undertaken.

The establishment of the blast furnaces

Backbarrow and Cunsey Furnaces, the first two charcoal-fired blast furnaces in Furness, were built in 1711–12. They were followed by Leighton Furnace in 1713, and (after quite an interval) the foundation of Nibthwaite and Duddon Furnaces in 1735–6 and 1737–8, Newland Furnace in 1746–7, Lowwood Furnace in 1747 and Penny Bridge Furnace in 1748. The founding partnerships, usually of between two and four men, were generally known by the eponymous name of the first blast furnace they founded. Three companies – Backbarrow, Cunsey and Newland – dominated the industry during the 18th century, establishing five of the eight blast furnaces and at one time or another having an interest in the remaining three. Each was also involved in a Scottish venture – Invergarry from 1727 until 1736, Bonawe from 1752–4 and Craleckan from about 1754. (The history of the blast furnaces is outlined in Chapter 1: A brief history of the industry) The Backbarrow Company was the most acquisitive of the three, building Backbarrow and Leighton Furnaces but also having an interest, sometimes short-lived and on occasion jointly with another company, in Cunsey, Duddon, Penny Bridge and Lowwood Furnaces. The Cunsey Company built two furnaces at Cunsey and (initially with the Backbarrow Company) at Duddon, while the Newland Company, named after Newland Furnace, grew out of the Nibthwaite Company. Four of the eight furnaces closed during the second half of the 18th century – Cunsey in 1750, Nibthwaite probably in about 1755 (although a forge ran until 1840), Penny Bridge in 1780 and Lowwood in 1785 – followed by Leighton in about 1806 and Craleckan in about 1813. Shortly afterwards, in 1818, Harrison, Ainslie and Company, lineal descendants of the Newland Company, took over the Backbarrow Company. In about 1828, they gained a monopoly in Furness by taking over the Company which ran both Duddon and Bonawe Furnaces. Duddon, Bonawe and Newland Furnaces closed between 1867 and 1891, but Backbarrow not until 1966.

Site topography

The blast furnaces in Furness were all water powered and built on valley-side sites close to the rivers and streams from which they drew their water supply. Buildings common to all sites were the blast furnace itself, one

or more iron-ore stores and charcoal barns, and some workers' housing. A number also had forges in which cast iron was converted to wrought iron. These had to be built where water power could be provided. The survival of buildings on the eight furnace sites varies, with substantial remains of all of them, either ruinous or converted in whole or part, at Backbarrow, Nibthwaite, Duddon and Newland, and storage buildings alone at Cunsey, Leighton, Lowwood and Penny Bridge.

The disposition of buildings on blast furnace sites was governed by local topography, that is, by the lie of the land and where water entered it and by how the buildings could best be sited in relation to each other. The weight of iron ore and the bulk of charcoal made their efficient delivery into storage buildings and the subsequent ease of their transfer to the blast furnace itself of particular importance. Every attempt was made to use the contours of the land to best effect.

Backbarrow Furnace (Fig 3.6 and *below*, Fig 3.34) is the most extensive of the Furness blast furnace sites and the one with the longest life. The blast furnace, fed by a headrace and a later pond taken off the River Leven, is sited at the foot of the valley side, below a road which divides the site and has all the storage buildings on its uphill side. All the latter buildings, namely two iron-ore stores and two separate charcoal barns, are therefore above the level of the charging house of the blast furnace and all used the natural slope to separate high-level loading from low-level unloading. An added stage in the evolution of these buildings came with the construction of the Lakeside and Haverthwaite branch line of the Furness Railway in 1869. Sidings off it caused alteration and rebuilding to an iron-ore store and a charcoal barn to allow direct unloading from railway wagons. The later development of the site saw a number of other industrial buildings constructed and changes made to existing ones. Backbarrow has a small surviving amount of housing.

Duddon Furnace, sited on rising ground on the western side of the Duddon Valley and fed by a headrace taken off the River Duddon (Fig 3.10), is a smaller site than Backbarrow but it is well planned with the considerable evolution of its storage buildings matched, as elsewhere, by the repair and renewal rather than replacement

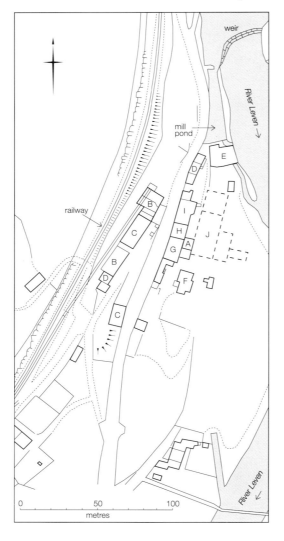

Figure 3.6
Backbarrow
Furnace: A blast
furnace, B ore stores,
C charcoal barn,
D housing, E forge,
later pug mill,
F blowing house,
G ovens, H roasting
house, I cupola
charging area,
J casting sheds.

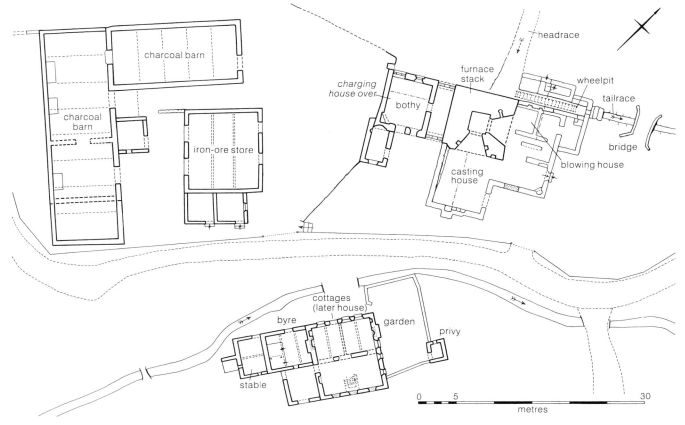

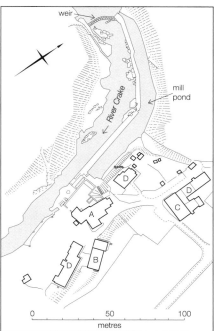

Figure 3.7 (above) Duddon Furnace, plan of buildings.

Figure 3.8 (far left) Duddon Furnace: view from the charcoal barn, with the ore store to right, towards the blast furnace (NMR BB97/09970).

Figure 3.9 (left) Nibthwaite Furnace: A furnace, B ore store, C charcoal barn, D housing.

of the blast furnace. The blast furnace, its waterwheel fed from a headrace with a right-angled turn against its outer wall, is sited at the lower end of an open yard (Fig 3.7) levelled up with slag and ash from the furnace. The tightly grouped cluster of storage buildings standing on the uphill side of the yard comprises two charcoal barns with four main periods of evolution in an L-shaped arrangement and an iron-ore store which replaces an earlier one. All these buildings were filled from a high level and emptied from a lower one slightly above the floor of the charging house of the blast furnace in an arrangement which made full use of natural slopes and gravity (Fig 3.8). The cottages on the site stand slightly apart from the industrial buildings.

Newland Furnace (Fig 3.11), not unlike Duddon and Backbarrow in its use of natural contours, stands at the mouth of a deep valley which cuts through the edge of the fells, its water supply taken from two mill ponds fed by the Newland Beck. The blast furnace itself stands at the foot of the valley slope into which its storage buildings are terraced at a slightly higher level. The iron-ore store, a single-phase structure, is level with the entrance to the charging house, but the charcoal barn complex, with four main stages of construction, stands slightly above it. As on some other furnace sites, there were for a time other associated industrial buildings, which made their own demands on the supply of water and charcoal. A refining forge was built on the site where the headrace left the original mill pond and worked from 1783 until 1807. In 1799 a rolling mill, later used as a blacking mill, was constructed just below the dam of the upper mill pond. As both buildings required charcoal for their forges and water for their bellows, their need for these is reflected on the site.

The blast furnaces at Cunsey, Leighton, Lowwood and Penny Bridge have all been demolished, but on all these sites storage buildings survive in some form and were either set level with the furnace or above it. Site topography dictated a less advantageous layout at Nibthwaite (Fig 3.9). The blast furnace there stands on the valley floor close to the River Crake, with the iron-ore store level with it but terraced into the valley side. The road up the valley originally passed the rear of this building and ore would have been emptied from carts directly into it through openings in its rear wall. The charcoal barn is on a terrace above the valley floor, gable-end on to the former road and a short distance from the other two industrial buildings. The siting of these storage buildings was such that when raw material was taken to the charging house of the blast furnace, the iron ore had to be barrowed up a considerable slope, while the

lighter but bulkier sacks of charcoal merely had to be led down a gentle slope. The earliest workers' housing on the site is next to the charcoal barn, with later housing built beyond the furnace and iron-ore store.

The buildings and water supply of the blast furnaces

Blast furnaces were complexes of buildings linked by a common process. Certain basic structural forms can be identified among the various buildings, but each evolved and expanded as necessary in response to commercial needs. The components of the blast furnace are examined below using a range of structural, documentary, carto-graphic and other visual evidence.

Water supply

The charcoal-fired blast furnaces in Furness, (with the exception of that at Backbarrow which from 1921 was blown by a steam engine) were all water powered. All had bellows which were operated by waterwheels; a number had refining forges and one a rolling mill, which required water power too. A sufficient and constant water supply had to be ensured, because when a blast furnace was in operation the blast ran continuously, the charge constantly replenished and the bellows always in use. Some idea of the demand for water comes from an appreciation that at Newland Furnace the six separate blasts between 1877 and closure in January 1891 varied in length from four to twenty-eight months.

The means of providing a reliable water supply varied, but the best served sites were those on major rivers which could be relied on both for a sufficient and constant supply. Weirs built across these diverted water into headraces, as on the River Leven at Backbarrow. The date of the construction of this weir is uncertain – John Machell took a lease in or before 1685 and erected a bloomforge on the site of an earlier bloomsmithy, building the blast furnace in 1711–12. A pond was later created to serve the forge. At Cunsey, Duddon, Lowwood and Penny Bridge, weirs divert water into long headraces, some of which broaden out in places to increase their capacity. The headrace at Duddon (Fig 3.10) is 690m long and leads directly to the blast furnace; its overflow was subsequently incorporated into that serving the adjacent but later bobbin mill.

The creation of mill ponds, their water held back by earth and rubble dams, provided a reserve of water where the natural supply was either minor or, particularly in summer, irregular. The supply to Leighton Furnace from the Leighton Beck was certainly minor, and a mill pond was created in the valley bottom with a headrace leading from it to the now demolished blast furnace. At Nibthwaite,

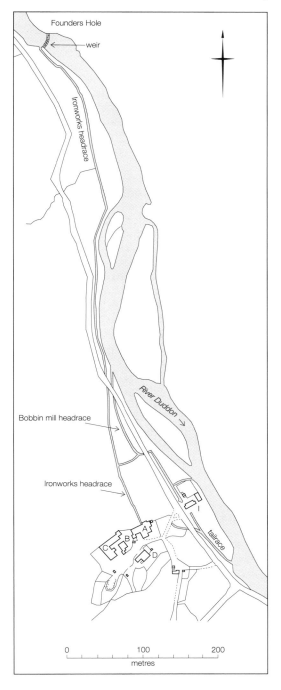

a plan surveyed in 1746 (*see* Fig 1.5) shows the original long, narrow pond created along one bank of the River Crake, immediately above the furnace. It also shows an incomplete enlargement of the pond, equivalent to that now on the site (*see* Fig 3.9), created to power the refining forge which finally opened in 1751, built out into the river at its downstream end and incorporating several former islands. At Newland Furnace (Fig 3.11) the short headrace to the blast furnace was taken off that to the medieval corn mill, which was fed from a pond created by building a weir across the Newland Beck. The extra call on water created by the erection of the blast furnace led to the construction of the upper mill pond higher up the valley. A lease of 1746 had granted the builders of the furnace the 'liberty of making a Dam and stopping or pounding the Water upon the same in the Watercourse a little above where the said Furnace is to be erected' (Fell 1908, 218).

The flow of water was converted into power by means of a wheel. A description of the original waterwheel at Leighton Furnace recorded its diameter as 'ten Yards [*c* 9m] within the Rim' (Ford and Fuller-Maitland 1931, 59), while the depiction of that at Nibthwaite on the 1746 plan (*see* Fig 1.5) shows a breastshot wheel, about 11.5m in diameter, set against the bridge house of the blast furnace and fed by a timber launder identified as 'The Trough which conveys the Water from the Dam to the Furnace Wheel'. On its closure in 1891, Newland had a high breastshot wheel some 39 feet (*c* 12m) in diameter. No complete waterwheel survives, although excavations at Duddon Furnace uncovered part of the pine frame of the last one there, a mid-19th-century shrouded wheel of low breast type with a diameter of over 8m. It stood within a cover building and scoremarks showed that an earlier wheel had been set at a slightly lower level.

The blast furnace

The blast furnace itself was a cluster of related buildings with the furnace at its core and a blowing house and its waterwheel, charging house and casting house attached to one or other side; at some sites there were other components, not necessarily all original, including a bothy, stores and office. Diderot shows external and internal views of a blast furnace and

Figure 3.10 Duddon Furnace: A furnace, B ore store, C charcoal barns, D housing.

these are an instructive comparison for the Furness blast furnaces (Gillespie 1959, plates 89 and 90). Four of the eight blast furnaces in Furness survive and two basic layouts can be identified: at Backbarrow and Duddon the associated structures are built against three of their sides, while at Nibthwaite and Newland, in a more compact arrangement, they abut just two. Since each pair of furnaces was founded by the same company, a preferred furnace layout might be suggested for each partnership. Although the buildings share many common features, however, the differing arrangements were in fact dictated by site topography. The builders of Duddon Furnace adopted the more compact layout when building Craleckan Furnace in Scotland, while the Newland Company built to the more extensive layout when constructing Bonawe Furnace.

The form of the early 18th-century blast furnaces

The blast furnace at Duddon, built in 1737–8, is one of the best preserved in the country, and many sources combine to provide unrivalled evidence of its form: a photograph of the 1890s (Fig 3.12), drawings reproduced by Alfred Fell (1908, frontispiece, opposite 209, 225 and 241), the surviving structure (Fig 3.13) and evidence from excavations. They are supported by a reconstruction drawing (see Fig 1.3). The furnace stack, typical of late charcoal-fired blast furnaces and of all those which survive in Furness, is a tower-like structure, square in plan, with sloping, battered lower walls to give solidity and resist distortion from heat. Above this, the 1890s photograph shows that a gallery ran around the top of the furnace, enclosing the wide square chimney over the mouth of the shaft inside. The gallery, lit and ventilated by small openings, was covered by a single-pitch roof which sloped up to the sides of the chimney and originally continued unbroken as the roof over the charging house which occupied the upper floor of the attached bridge house. The furnace stack, like all the buildings on the site (and indeed like virtually all the buildings on the eight blast furnace sites), is built of stone rubble. It has wide round-headed openings in two adjacent walls, one the blowing arch, the other the casting arch, the sides and tops of which taper into the furnace. Much of the blowing arch, however, has been rebuilt in a different form after collapse. The furnace shaft within the stack has a square base which originally contained the hearth and the crucible into which the molten iron and slag settled as the blast proceeded. The shaft above this area is now bulbous in section and circular in plan, its lining, called the 'inwall' in 18th-century documents, composed of firebricks and a renewal of mid-19th-century date.

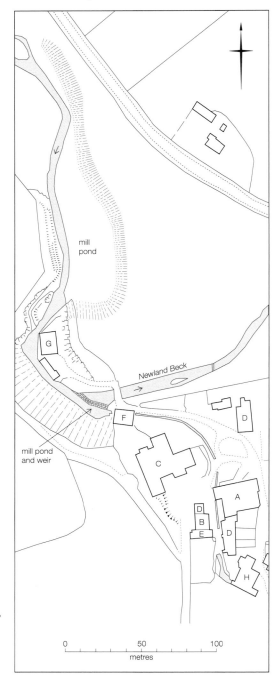

Figure 3.11
Newland Furnace:
A furnace, B ore store,
C charcoal barns,
D housing, E office,
F forge, G rolling mill,
H corn mill.

At the top of the shaft, a door opened from the charging house into the chimney level with the charging mouth of the furnace, the square chimney rising above it to draw off the smoke and fumes.

The bridge house, which abutted the west side of the stack and included the charging house, was so named because it spanned from ground level to a high level on the furnace stack. It is a two-storey building,

Figure 3.12 Duddon Furnace: photograph of the blast furnace and associated buildings taken in the 1890s. (Mrs Meryl Barker)

Figure 3.13 Duddon Furnace: blast furnace from the east (NMR BB99/06647).

originally gabled at its outer end, which contained a bothy for furnace workmen heated by a fireplace on its ground floor. It was originally separated from the furnace by an insulation void. The first floor was occupied for its full length by the charging house, whose sloping timber floor led up to the top of the furnace. The iron ore, charcoal and flux, the raw materials required for the charge, were brought from the storage buildings on the site and assembled here before being carried in baskets, in appropriate quantities and in the appropriate order, up to the furnace mouth and cast into the furnace. Windows lighting the charging house were few, as at other blast furnaces.

The blowing house, a tall gabled single-storey building attached to the east side of the furnace, now reduced to its footings, contained a pair of bellows which were driven by the waterwheel attached to its outer side. The original bellows, which would have been the traditional concertina bellows of wood and leather, as well as the original waterwheel, have both been replaced. The roof of this building originally extended down over a room which provided a link between the blowing house and the casting house. Heaton Cooper's watercolour (Fell 1908, plate opposite 209) shows that the party wall between the blowing house and the corner room had a tall voussoired quadrant arch. The latter

room, with its corner fireplace, was evidently used by men involved with the smelting. The casting house on the south side of the stack, itself another tall, gabled single-storey building now also reduced to its footings, was revealed by excavation to have had a casting pit along the full length of one wall, filled to a depth of about 400mm with firm yellow sand.

The blast furnace at Backbarrow, the first to be completed in Furness but now much altered after changes in 1870 and 1921, seems originally to have been not unlike Duddon in its arrangement. It is now reduced to the battered stone walls of the lower part of the original square furnace stack. The sides of the two original openings into the casting house and blowing house survive in adjacent walls, however (although with renewed lintels and heads), as does the wheelpit for the waterwheel against the rear face of the blowing house. A watercolour by William Fell, dated 1908 but entitled 'Backbarrow Furnace in 1850' (Fell 1908, plate opposite 209), appears to be an accurate representation of the blast furnace at that date, indicating that the bridge house was on the opposite side of the stack to the blowing house and roofed in continuation with the gallery roof in the customary manner.

The reasons for the arrangement of the buildings attached to three sides of the furnaces at Duddon and Backbarrow are

Figure 3.14 Nibthwaite Furnace: blast furnace with bobbin mill over, from the west (NMR BB97/02162).

clear: they are the result of matching the flow of materials and the sequence of processes to the reality of site topography, in particular the opposing pulls of water at the lower end of the site and the higher land above it on which the storage buildings were constructed. Site topography, however, enabled a more compact building arrangement to be adopted for the blast furnaces at both Nibthwaite and Newland. At each site there was a furnace stack, the bridge house on one side incorporating a charging house over a blowing house. The latter had a waterwheel attached to one side and a casting house on an adjacent side. The furnace stacks were like those at Backbarrow and Duddon, with a battered stone lower part surmounted by a gallery and central chimney: both are now incomplete.

Nibthwaite Furnace (Fig 3.14) was built in 1735–6 but the construction of a bobbin mill in the early 1840s removed the top half of the stack and the whole of the charging house. The original appearance of the building is, however, known from its depiction on the 1746 plan (Fig 1.5) which shows a conventional furnace stack with battered lower part, gallery and projecting central chimney. The gallery roof runs on as the roof of the bridge house, itself shown with windows into the charging house and a large waterwheel against its outside wall. The casting house is shown as a single-storey block projecting from the rear. The surviving parts of the original blast furnace are clearly recognisable externally (Fig 3.14). Inside, the stone furnace stack (Fig 3.15) has openings into the blowing house and casting house, both tapering and formerly identical with segmental outer and inner arches, all with rubble voussoirs and shallow rubble

vaults sloping down between them. The inner arches are supported by original cast-iron lintels cast with the inscription 'N 1736' in relief. The outer arch to the casting house remains, supported by an arched cast-iron lintel inserted under it. The other arch collapsed, however, and has timber beams in its place. The square masonry surrounding the hearth at the base of the furnace shaft survives, but not the hearth. The surviving part of the shaft tapers gently and is square in plan with convex sides, its lining constructed of finely cut ashlar-like blocks of sandstone (Fig 3.16). The structure of the boshes (which taper in at the base of the shaft to feed the charge into the hearth) have been lost, but their position is indicated by the curved lower edges of a green vitrified deposit on all four sides of the lining of the shaft. The original blowing house survives, with later internal features on its floor, but a tall and wide archway opens into the space at its rear, which links through to the former casting house. The latter, like those known on several other sites, had two rooms, one now lost.

Newland Furnace was built in 1746–7 and the blast furnace (Fig 3.17) survives in a tolerably complete state, although the original gallery and chimney were lost when the latter was rebuilt in 1874. A photograph of the site taken in the mid-1890s (see Fig 3.19), shortly after its closure, shows this new chimney as well as other buildings, but much has since been lost. The battered base of the stone furnace stack survives but the two openings through it into the

Figure 3.15 Nibthwaite Furnace: blast furnace.

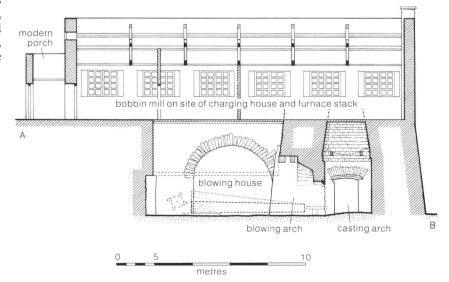

*Figure 3.16
Nibthwaite Furnace:
interior of blast
furnace shaft (NMR
AA97/02120).*

*Figure 3.17
Newland Furnace:
blast furnace.*

house on the ground floor, a bothy, entered through a doorway in a corner away from the furnace contrived in its upper part and the charging house, later extended, over it. The waterwheel was against an outer wall. It is likely that workers, including perhaps some of the men who led charcoal to the site, slept in the bothy. Its floor, which no longer survives, was probably removed when the present stone bases and timber cross beams were inserted to support new cylinder bellows. The casting house, still roofed in the mid-1890s, is now a roofless shell. It originally had two rooms with arched openings between them, the room opening off the furnace having a sand floor for casting the pig iron.

Alterations to the blast furnaces
Blast furnaces were subject to considerable stresses during their periods in blast, but the furnace stacks at their core and the buildings attached to them stood the test of time. Apart from necessary repair and renewal, they were in general not subject to the major extensions or replacements which typify the storage buildings.

The furnace stacks are all substantially built of stone rubble, but a weak point in some lay in the construction of the blowing and casting arches. At Duddon and Nibthwaite these were round and segmental in shape, but some failed and either had to be supported by inserted cast-iron lintels or replaced (*see* Fig 3.13). The furnace shafts themselves, however, were subject to the greatest stresses of extremes of heat, and

blowing house and the casting house, which taper in plan and have flat stepped vaults, each have renewed outer arches. The square masonry at the base of the stack surrounding the former hearth also survives, as does part of some early freestone lining, identical in shape to that at Nibthwaite but largely hidden by the later shaft lining. The bridge house was a composite building, with the blowing

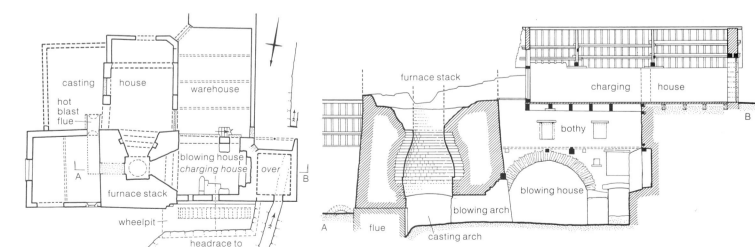

after they were blown out it was necessary to rebuild the hearths and reline shafts. At Duddon, 18th-century account books include a number of references to the purchase of the hearthstones which stood at the base of the shaft. What appears to have been quite major building work on the furnace took place in 1759–60 (Lancashire Record Office, DDX 192/2-3). In August 1759, freestone was bought for the 'inwalls' of the furnace; by 26 October, a labourer had spent 33 days 'pulling out Hearth and Inwalls etc'. Continuing payments to masons and for freestone until January 1760 point to its complete relining. On 5 February 1760, the bottom stone of the hearth was laid and after other work, including cleaning and 'gearing' the bellows, the furnace was blown in on 22 March. The freestone lining of the shaft at Duddon is no longer visible, but, as noted above, those at Nibthwaite (*see* Fig 3.16) and Newland remain, both convex-sided squares in section and tapering in profile. At Newland the freestone is largely hidden by a later firebrick lining. Firebricks became the usual lining material during the 19th century and the purchase of bricks for the tunnel head at Duddon

Figure 3.18 Duddon Furnace: interior of blast furnace shaft (NMR AA98/13926).

in 1774 is therefore an early use of them. At the very beginning of the 19th century, Rees was able to record bricks as a recent introduction (Cossons 1972, **3**, 159, 163–4)

Figure 3.19 Newland Furnace: mid-1890s photograph from the North Lonsdale Magazine, October 1897.

Figure 3.20 Backbarrow Furnace: blast furnace shaft from the south in 1994 (NMR AA94/03010).

and to note the move to circular-sectioned shafts in coke-fuelled furnaces. These were also adopted by the charcoal-fired furnaces in Furness, as the mid- and later 19th-century circular-sectioned and bulbous profiles of firebrick-lined interiors of the shafts at Duddon (Fig 3.18) and Newland indicate. These later linings fit awkwardly on the square shapes of the hearths below. Relining shafts was more usual than rebuilding stacks: the interior of the shaft at Backbarrow has been lost but Fell's claim (1908, 208) that the stack was pulled down and rebuilt in 1770 is questionable and may be an error for the substantial remodelling which took place in 1870 when two new openings were cut through it and a new lintel cast with that date was inserted. Rebuilding might have been necessary had there been an explosion. Diderot wrote that there was no defence against the danger of explosion – 'For workmen and plant alike, eruptions are the most terrible danger. They bring death to those nearby and spread fire far and wide. In a sudden explosion, a furnace will throw up all its contents, molten and solid. It becomes a volcano vomiting flame fragments from every opening'. If workers should see the furnace gasping in this way, 'flight is the most expedient measure'

(Gillespie 1959, **1**, text to plate 87). The blast furnace at Leighton, whose lease was taken in 1755 by the Halton Company of Lancaster and which closed in about 1806, is said to have blown up and never to have been rebuilt (Fell 1908, 210).

There were inevitably changes to the timber waterwheels at the blast furnaces: excavations, as noted earlier, have indicated something of this at Duddon. There were also changes to the bellows which the waterwheels drove. Inevitably, the original concertina bellows wore out and had to be repaired or renewed, but some time after 1780, perhaps in 1790, the industry switched over to blowing cylinders. These survived until the early 20th century and are shown by Fell (Fell 1908, opposite 241).

Such cylinders had been pioneered in the forge at Backbarrow in 1737 by Isaac Wilkinson, but the company had not thought it wise at this time to install larger versions of them in the new furnace at Duddon. They were later installed in the forges at Newland and Lowwood and in the furnaces at Lowwood and Backbarrow.

The greatest changes made to the Furness blast furnaces in the 19th century were at Newland and Backbarrow, where their operators, Harrison, Ainslie and Company, installed coke smelting with the hot blast system – the hot waste gases from the furnace mouth were directed into pre-heating a stove, which then heated the original cold blast. The system had been pioneered in 1829 by J B Nielson of Glasgow, on the proposition that output would increase and economies be made in fuel consumption. After 1857, however, it was superseded by regenerative stoves developed by E A Cowper (Trinder 1992, 184, 336–7). The hot blast system at Newland was installed in 1874, the mid-1890s photograph (Fig 3.19) showing that the shaft was raised in order to increase draught by means of a brick tower with a gabled top, a side chimney rising through the side of the stack and up one side of the tower. These additions have now gone. The furnace stack at Backbarrow (Fig 3.20) has undergone considerable change. It was remodelled in 1870 and in 1921, when its upper part was rebuilt in brick on conversion to coke firing. A steam engine was also installed to blow air into the hearth and the casting house was replaced with a large shed. A coke-fired cupola furnace was installed to recycle scrap metal during the 1950s.

Iron-ore stores

Since iron ore had to be kept dry before being added to the charge in the furnace, buildings in which it could be stored had to be provided. Iron ore – sometimes called 'mine' in documents, and the stores 'minehouses' – is not especially large in its mass but it is heavy, and this influenced both the form and siting of the stores. Most were terraced into slopes to allow ore to be directly off-loaded from carts through high-level openings in the rear wall and then taken out through low-level doorways in the front wall. Gravity aided the delivery and unloading of ore. At all sites but Nibthwaite, the stores were built at or above the level of the entrance to the charging house of the blast furnace, so that minimum effort was required to move it there.

Obtaining sufficient iron ore was not a problem. Consequently, the surviving iron-ore stores are almost all single-phase buildings without the enlargement characteristic of the barns in which charcoal was stored. They are all single-storey buildings, which vary in height, and their walls and often the ground around them are stained red from the iron in the hematite ore. At Leighton and Nibthwaite, sites with relatively short lives as blast furnaces, but also at Newland, a site with a far longer life, it is likely that the iron-ore stores are the original ones. That at Lowwood has been subject to some rebuilding and at Duddon, the original iron-ore store was replaced by a new one, probably during the 19th century. Two were built at Backbarrow, a reflection perhaps of the consolidation of work there by Harrison, Ainslie and Company, the southern store being earlier than the northern one.

Iron-ore stores are of two types, with interiors which were either divided into compartments or open throughout. Leighton, Newland and the northern iron-ore store at Backbarrow have divided interiors. The Leighton ore store, known from an ink sketch (Fig 3.21), had a single-pitch roof and either three or four compartments: four unloading doors are shown but just two stone dividing walls. No rear loading doors are depicted. The ore store at Newland, now altered but set in a

Figure 3.21 Leighton Furnace: undated drawing of the ore store (Cumbria Record Office, Barrow, BDX/215).

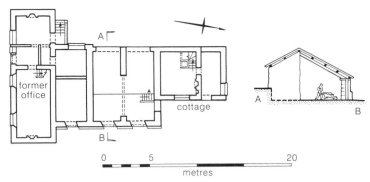

*Figure 3.22 Newland
Furnace: ore store,
office and cottage.*

*Figure 3.23 Backbarrow
Furnace: railway line
passing coke store and
entering ore store
(Andrew Lowe).*

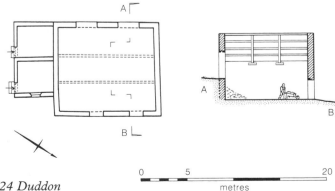

*Figure 3.24 Duddon
Furnace: ore store.*

range with a contemporary office and cottage (Fig 3.22), has three compartments, each with its own high-level rear loading door and front door for unloading. The latter doorways have angled sides to ease barrowing the ore to the furnace. The Backbarrow ore store (Fig 3.23) straddles the railway siding, the railway lines passing through it to enable ore to be emptied through the bottom of railway wagons. The compartment arrangement had several advantages, particularly the ability to segregate ores from different sources or – if necessary – to separate unwashed or uncalcined ore from the rest or to keep flux separate from the ore. The evidence of the Swedish metallurgist Gustav Ekman, who visited Newland on 27 December 1828, indicates that the rich local hematite ore was mixed with poorer ore from Wales or Staffordshire at the rate of one basket of the latter to four and a half hundredweight of local ore (Nils Ekman personal communication). The compartments on the site would have enabled these to be kept separate until the mixing took place.

The iron-ore stores with undivided interiors are the southern one at Backbarrow and others at Nibthwaite, Duddon and Lowwood. The Duddon ore store, probably of early 19th-century date, is a tall nearly-square building with a pitched roof which is clearly shown on the 1890s photograph (*see* Fig 3.12) to have been recently heightened. It is terraced into the hillside and has pairs of doors in its front and rear walls, the latter opening on to a drop to the cobbled floor (Fig 3.24). The arrangement of the other ore stores is less certain. That at Nibthwaite is shown on the 1746 plan with the single-pitch roof it still possesses, although the rear wall has been reduced in height, losing the original loading openings off the former road (Fig 1.5). The two doorways in the front wall, though modified, are likely to reflect the original arrangement. The Backbarrow ore store, later used as a scrap house, seems to have had three high-level rear openings, but the front wall has been largely removed.

Charcoal barns

Obtaining and storing adequate supplies of charcoal, confusingly called 'coal' in contemporary documents, were crucial to the running of blast furnaces and their associated forges and considerable effort had to be put into obtaining it. The rivals of the Newland Company, for example, were successful in securing command of much the greater part of the wood available for charcoal making in the district during the 18th century. In about 1780 the company also began to buy woods in Scotland and to erect storehouses on the coast of Galloway for the storage of charcoal awaiting shipment to Furness. Many journeys were made to Galloway 'to look for woods' (Fell 1908, 137). The three companies subsequently came to an agreement over the supply of charcoal.

Charcoal was friable and fairly easily crushed or shaken to powder, either in transport or storage. Some wastage must have been allowed for and indeed a proposal to export Galloway charcoal by sea to Furness in the late 18th century freely acknowledged that about one quarter of the intended cargo would not be usable on arrival. Carriage by packhorse was probably even more wasteful. Charcoal was transported and stored in sacks and frequently delivered in dozens. A contract made in Scotland in 1752 for charcoal for the Bonawe furnace defined a dozen of charcoal as 'twelve Baggs or Sack-full, the Dimensions of each sack being two yards and a half English in length and one yard in Breadth within between seam and seam when empty, to be filled in the Woods so that the Coal may be four feet ten inches high when fairly sett down by the Carrier and Stocktaker at the said Furnace' (Fell 1908, 393). Such close

definition was important for all parties since many wood owners maintained grievances about the price ironmasters paid for charcoal. In 1748 Myles Sandys, Furness wood-owner and a founding partner in Penny Bridge Furnace, complained of 'the excess of measure' insisted upon by the ironmasters, which made his and others' 'Woods of much less value than they formerly were. The sacks or bags they imposed were some four or five inches wider than common, and they insisted on their being filled five feet high, by which means the bags contained nearly one-fourth more than usual' (Fell 1908, 145).

Charcoal barns, called coal-houses in some documents, were built to store charcoal and, as was vital, to keep it dry. They survive on every one of the eight blast furnace sites. At Cunsey there are merely fragments of masonry, but elsewhere they are generally near-complete, albeit some roofless and others converted. At Leighton, Nibthwaite, Lowwood and Penny Bridge, sites with comparatively short working lives or where demand was not excessive, the original charcoal barns survive unextended and evidently unaltered during the ironworking period. Elsewhere, on what were the principal furnaces of each of the three main companies, extra storage capacity had to be provided. At Backbarrow, two separate charcoal barns were constructed during the life of the furnace, while at Duddon and Newland, the original barns were retained as the core of multi-phase accretive complexes.

Figure 3.25 Nibthwaite Furnace: charcoal barn prior to its conversion to a house (Mike Davies-Shiel).

*Figure 3.26
Backbarrow
Furnace: north
charcoal barn, later
a coke store.*

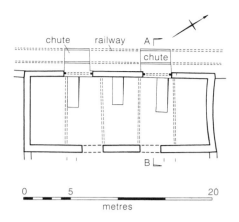

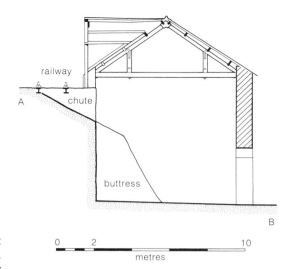

The charcoal barn at Nibthwaite, built when the site was founded in 1735–6 and used initially for the furnace and then for the forge until this closed in 1840, was subsequently modified slightly to store wood for the bobbin mills and saw mill established on the site. It is now a house but in its original form, known from its depiction on the 1746 plan (Fig 1.5) and a pre-conversion photograph (Fig 3.25), it was a tall gabled building, rectangular in plan and probably with openings only in its front wall. The original ground-floor door still survives, but little is known about higher-level openings apart from a gabled taking-in door set centrally in the front roof slope. This is shown on the 1746 drawing and although it has disappeared externally, internally a break in the roof purlins confirms that it existed and presumably enabled a hoist to raise sacks of charcoal into the building. The interior was probably an open space with some form of timber flooring or racking provided to store the sacks of charcoal conveniently but without risk of crushing. Slits or small openings in gable walls were the usual means of ventilating the interiors of charcoal barns. The 1746 drawing shows some high up in the gable wall. The charcoal barns at Leighton, Lowwood and Penny Bridge are gabled rectangular stone buildings like that at Nibthwaite, although they are all larger than it, and those at Lowwood and Penny Bridge are terraced into the slope, enabling sacks to be offloaded at the rear.

At Backbarrow, the north and south charcoal barns were built before 1846–8, and it is likely that the north building (Fig 3.26) is the earlier one, sited as it is in between the two iron-ore stores and closer to the blast furnace. It is a long rectangular building with two openings on two levels in its front wall, altered when it became a coke store on the changeover from charcoal to coke in 1921. The rear wall was raised and two wide loading chutes, protected by framed gabled roofs (*see* Fig 3.23), were created to enable the coke to be tipped directly from railway wagons. The south charcoal store, the smaller of the two though as tall, has single centrally set high- and low-level openings, the latter doorway opening directly on to the road. The construction of these separate charcoal barns at Backbarrow was the consequence of the restrictive nature of a site on which the buildings were spread out along a fairly steep valley side divided both by a public road and a railway. The constraints of the site, combined with the inevitably *ad hoc* growth of the site over such a long period – with extra buildings constructed as need arose – prevented the more efficient expansion exhibited by the charcoal barns at Duddon and Newland Furnaces.

The charcoal barns at Duddon are set in an L shape, encompassing the iron-ore store, and have a four-stage evolution (Fig 3.27). The original charcoal barn of 1737–8, rectangular in plan, was terraced into the slope above the blast furnace. A second charcoal barn, divided by a cross wall and larger than the original one, was built across the rear of the latter, over its loading area. After a disastrous fire, this second barn was substantially rebuilt, the opportunity being taken to extend it and to add a front annexe. The final stage of evolution saw the original barn raised to the height of its neighbour. The successive barns were all gabled structures with tall interiors (Fig 3.28), whose walls give no

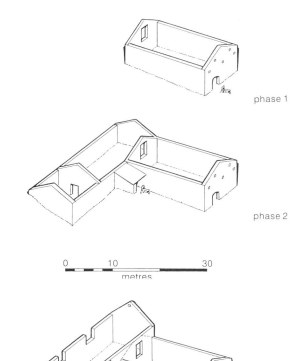

phase 1

phase 2

0   10   30
metres

phase 3

phase 4
(buttresses later)

slope, parallel with the road to the rear. Two further barns being added before 1846, one to its north-east beyond an added lean-to range, perhaps built in the early 1780s, and one to the south, now demolished. A fourth barn, the largest of them all, was built between 1846 and 1888, perhaps in the 1850s or 1860s. It was the only one to be built into rather than along the slope. The first three barns were discrete buildings which were linked by internal doorways, but the fourth barn opened completely into the first, its roof continuing on through the original building to a gable wall, raised on top of the eaves of the original building and containing a tall taking-in door linked by a bridge to the public road behind the site.

Figure 3.27 Duddon Furnace: development diagram of the charcoal barns.

Figure 3.28 Duddon Furnace: interior of the second charcoal barn, from the south-east. (NMR BB97/09980)

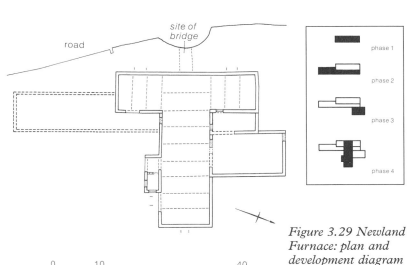

Figure 3.29 Newland Furnace: plan and development diagram of the charcoal barns.

indication of the fixed staging which the sacks of fragile charcoal would have required and which seems to be indicated by the high-level loading doors found in all uphill walls. The first and second barns each had a single unloading door in the wall facing the blast furnace, that of the second barn protected by a roofed porch; a second doorway was inserted into the front wall of the later barn when it was extended after the fire.

The charcoal barns at Newland have a more complex evolution than those at Duddon, in which four principal buildings can be identified (Fig 3.29). The original charcoal barn of 1746–7 was built along the

This final addition massively increased the storage capacity of charcoal at the site, perhaps indicating that it was built at a time of consolidation by Harrison, Ainslie and Company. Loading and unloading of the barns made good use of the valley slope, with loading doors off a terrace behind the original barn and the high-level bridge already noted. The latter merely continued an existing delivery point into the building. Unloading doors out of the barns seem to have been kept to a minimum, but the position of one in the rear gable of the north-east barn is significant. This door opens on to a trackway which leads to the forge, now a cottage, which operated on the site between 1783 and 1807; it seems likely that this new charcoal barn was built to store charcoal intended for use in the forge. The extra capacity of the enlarged charcoal barns can be appreciated if it is realised that the original barn at Duddon had a capacity, crudely measured to eaves level, of 600m³, which increased to a final 2,000m³. At Newland the equivalent figures are 1,400m³ and 5,000m³.

Forges and foundries

The conversion of pig iron to wrought iron was carried out in refining forges which were either on the blast furnace sites or were quite independent of them (*see below*, Forges). The forge hearths were charcoal fired and their bellows, as well as their tilt hammers, were water powered. On-site forges were thus in potential conflict with blast furnaces in their need for fuel and power. The need for fuel was perhaps the least problematical since wherever the forge was sited, charcoal had to be found; the only requirement was sufficient storage space. Too little is known about most sites for this aspect to be taken further, but it is significant that at Newland it seems that one of the charcoal barns was built where it could serve the forge, opened in 1783, and subsequently the rolling mill of 1799. The call on water had more potential for disrupting blast furnaces, given the long periods over which smelting campaigns ran and during which the bellows had to work continuously. On a site such as Backbarrow, on a major river, there was probably little problem with water supply, but at Nibthwaite, the mill pond had to be enlarged before the forge opened in 1751. At Newland, the forge was sited on the headrace which led to

the blast furnace and the corn mill, but at Lowwood, documents seem to imply a separate headrace from the furnace (Fell 1908, 220).

All eight blast furnaces produced pig iron, and at one time or another at least five of them, Backbarrow, Leighton, Nibthwaite, Duddon and Newland, also produced cast-iron wares. Backbarrow is the only site known to have had a separate foundry and it must be presumed that at the others the objects which were cast, ranging from domestic ironwork of all types to cannon and shot, were produced in moulds in the casting houses attached to the furnaces.

The rolling mill and blacking mill at Newland

According to Fell (1908, 218), the first and only mill building introduced into the district for rolling bars of iron was installed in 1799, although its production was not received with favour and it evidently closed in the early 19th century. Rolling mills had several sets of rolls, rotated at Newland by water power, in which iron was

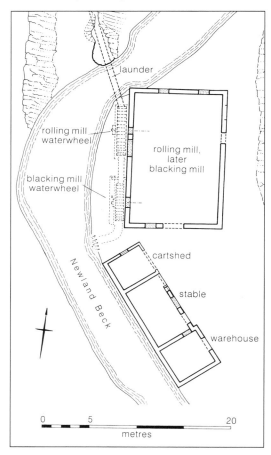

Figure 3.30 Newland Furnace: rolling mill, later converted to a blacking mill.

elongated and formed into particular shapes, according to the profile of the rolls. Rounds, squares, angles, plates, sheets and other sections could have been produced (Trinder 1992, 633). The rolling mill at Newland was at the north end of the site, immediately below the dam of the upper mill pond (Fig 3.30). The building, later used for other purposes, is a broad rectangle in plan but is now reduced to low rubble walls. There is evidence for water power in the form of blocked openings for the axles of two waterwheels in the west wall, one perhaps to drive the rolls, one the bellows of the hearth in which the iron was reheated prior to rolling. The interior of a rolling mill is shown by Diderot (Gillespie 1959, **1**, plate 99), and a description and detailed drawings in Rees (Cossons 1959, **2**, 323–9 and **4**, *Iron Manufacture*, plates I–V).

It is not known when the rolling mill ceased working, but by the middle of the 19th century, certainly before 1844 when it first burned out, the building was a blacking mill. The waste incurred during the transport of charcoal has already been noted, but this could be put to use as blacking, a fine charcoal powder used to line moulds in order to put a good skin on castings, as well as for shoe blacking and later for water filters. A lease of 1862 describes 'All that Blacking Mill with . . . Troughs Water Wheel Shafts Head Stock Framing and premises', referring to the 'inside Machinery Gearing and Fittings' and specifies that Harrison, Ainslie and Company would sell to the blacking manufacturer, to be ground in the mill, all the charcoal slack provided by the company at their iron furnace at Newland. If the quantity was insufficient, the slack would be supplied from their iron furnaces at Backbarrow or Duddon. The 'Trough' was the timber launder which took water from the upper mill pond across the beck and down the side of the building at eaves level to feed a single overshot waterwheel at its south end. The blacking mill is likely to have closed when the furnace ceased working in 1891, after which the building became a sawmill and then farm buildings.

Figure 3.31 Duddon Furnace: cottages opposite the blast furnace (NMR AA98/13932).

Housing

The eight early 18th-century blast furnaces were all built, by virtue of their need for water power and charcoal, in rural situations and, rather like the equivalent late 18th- and early 19th-century textile mills, those that survived evolved as industrial hamlets. The early dates of foundation make them of especial interest and because the industry that they served did not require a very large workforce, they remained comparatively small settlements.

Housing was required for the men who ran the blast furnaces. At Leighton these included a stocktaker's house and founder's house (Fell 1908, 210), while at Duddon, documents refer to a chief furnaceman, or keeper, and there were also the labourers who handled the charcoal and iron ore, a stocktaker, the fillers responsible for charging the furnace and the men who supervised the bellows and assisted with the casting process (Marshall 1984). Not everyone necessarily lived on site. Duddon lacks much housing: the cottages opposite the blast furnace (*see* Fig 3.7) originated in the late 18th or early 19th century simply as a pair of single-fronted cottages, one room deep and two storeys high (Fig 3.31). They were later extended to the rear and had a byre and a loose box added to the side. Some men may have lived in the bothy in the furnace complex while it was in blast, but otherwise most of the workers must have lived off-site.

Closure of furnaces, site development and redevelopment have all taken their toll of buildings, but among the most interesting sites, with some of the earliest surviving workers' housing in the country, are the hamlets of Low Nibthwaite and Lowwood. Both grew up as a result of the establishment of blast furnaces in 1735–6 and 1747. At Nibthwaite, the row of houses (Fig 3.32) attached to the charcoal barn can be equated with the range of two-storey buildings depicted on the 1746 plan of the site (*see* Fig 1.5), surveyed barely a decade after the furnace was built. The isolated cottage in front of the charcoal barn also survives, although subsequently extended, and further housing was built on the valley floor before the closure of the forge in 1840 (*see* Fig 3.9). At Lowwood, a terrace of four two-storey single-fronted cottages, later extended, could well have originated as the cottages which it is known the founding company built for its workers. Additions to it probably date from the era of the Gunpowder Works which succeeded the iron furnace. When it was put up for sale in 1852, Backbarrow Ironworks included a manager's cottage, other cottages and workmen's houses, although few of these can be identified on site. At Newland (Fig 3.33), however, an impressive row of two and three-storey dwellings of 18th- and early 19th-century date includes a former ironmaster's house.

Figure 3.32 Nibthwaite Furnace: cottages and former charcoal barn, now a house, from the south-west (NMR BB97/02167).

*Figure 3.33
Newland Furnace:
housing next to blast
furnace, from the
east (NMR
BB97/10034).*

Forges

Pig iron produced by the blast furnace was converted into wrought iron in the charcoal-fired finery forge. There were three elements of a forge – the finery hearth, the chafery hearth and the tilt hammer – all of which used water power. A forge commonly had two fineries to one chafery, an arrangement which reflected the relative output of each type of hearth. In the finery hearth, the pig was melted under a blast of air, removing the residual carbon in the iron and allowing a 'loup' of wrought iron to form. This was removed and hammered into an ancony (see Chapter 1: A note on terminology). There were no further chemical changes to the iron in the chafery; the ancony was simply reheated and shaped into bars. The bar iron was sold to blacksmiths, but at Newland some was utilised by a short-lived rolling mill to produce shaped-section bars (*see above*, this chapter: The rolling mill and blacking mill at Newland).

The processes of refining and direct smelting followed a similar series of steps and there was probably little structural difference between the finery forges and the bloomforges which preceded them (Awty and Phillips 1980, 25). The early history of the finery forge in Furness may be, in part, a reflection of these similarities; the bloomforges at Cunsey, Backbarrow, Spark Bridge, Coniston, Force, Hacket and Burblethwaite were all working as refining forges shortly after the construction of the blast furnaces at Backbarrow and Cunsey in 1711–12.

Backbarrow and Cunsey became the early foci of forging activities because of their proximity to the newly built furnaces. In contrast, the off-site forges at Hacket and Burblethwaite were short-lived, ceasing work during the early 1720s. Stony Hazel forge, built in 1718–19 was jointly acquired by the Backbarrow and Cunsey Companies in 1724–5 but remained unused thereafter and Coniston and Force Forge both closed in 1744. Their abandonment suggests that the ironmasters regarded these particular sites as too distant from the furnaces to be of use – while their needs could be adequately served by closer forges. Spark Bridge was probably saved from a similar fate by its situation on the River Crake and was worked in succession by the Cunsey, Backbarrow and Newland Companies from 1715 to 1848 . The forge at Cunsey closed at the same time as the blast furnace in 1750. Despite the fall-off in the number of working forges during the first half of the 18th century, the leases of the disused sites were commonly retained by the different companies to forestall any competition. The crucial factor affecting the provision of forges was the amount of pig iron that was exported from the region and sold to independent foundries and forges. All of the Furness ironmasters supplied pig iron to forges operated by the Knight Stour partnership in the Midlands at various times between 1740 and 1796 (Riden 1993, 107–20). The quantities of pig iron exported to other regions could be significant; in 1713–15 the Backbarrow company sent two-thirds of its output of pig iron to operators in Bristol and the Midlands

(Raistrick 1968, 99). Cast goods were also manufactured at some of the blast furnaces, but this never amounted to a large proportion of their output.

It did not always make economic sense, therefore, to build or maintain a finery beside each furnace, since any remaining pig iron could be readily transported to a separate finery. Thus Duddon and Penny Bridge Furnaces were never provided with on-site forges and a significant number of those forges which were built alongside the furnaces were only operational for a fraction of the furnace's working life. Duddon Furnace in particular was intended to supply the Midlands forges and remained peripheral to the network of forges in Furness. At Nibthwaite a forge was built in 1751, only about four years before the furnace was blown out, but continued working until 1840. A forge operated at Newland between 1783 and 1807, its short life probably due to the company's ability to use its sister site at Nibthwaite. A forge was built at Lowwood in the later 18th century, but dismantled in 1785 (Fell 1908, 220).

The form of no on-site refining forge is known for certain: that at Nibthwaite – evidently at the south end of the enlarged mill pond – was later occupied by a saw mill, now demolished, while at Newland the forge is now a cottage which straddles the headrace. The site of the finery at Lowwood is unknown. Only at Backbarrow are there some remains which can be tentatively interpreted *see below*, Backbarrow forges). Some indication of their appearance can be gained from contemporary illustrations (Gillespie 1959, 1, plates 95-8; Cossons 1972, 3, plates I–II; Fig 3.37).

Paradoxically, those sites which were abandoned earliest have generally survived best. Hacket and Stony Hazel both operated as bloomforges for most of their lives. Stony Hazel is a particularly enigmatic site, which was probably designed to refine iron but may never have done so during its short life (*see below*, Stoney Hazel, Rusland). It is particularly valuable as a rare survival of the hearth itself and the associated buildings, including a charcoal barn. At Hacket, little remains of the forge buildings, but the water management system is a fine example of its kind. There are still remains of the forge at Cunsey, and the 'Pugmill' at Backbarrow has been identfied as a possible former forge.

Cunsey forge

The earliest reference to a bloomforge at Cunsey is an agreement made in 1623 to purchase woods in order to secure an ample supply of charcoal for its use. The forge was in the hands of William Rawlinson or John Machell prior to the formation of the Backbarrow Company in 1711, when it became one of that company's concerns. On the expiry of their lease in 1715, the forge stopped work and the lease was taken over by the rival Cunsey Company. They reconstructed the forge and worked it as a refinery in conjunction with their furnace, a short distance downstream. On the expiry of this lease in 1750, both sites came into the hands of the Backbarrow Company; neither was worked again – the forge was partly dismantled in 1760 and demolished in 1800 (Fell 1908, 191–3).

The forge stands on the Cunsey Beck and comprises a silted-up pond created by building a 2m-high dam across the valley bottom. The stream has broken through this towards its northern end, but close to its southern end is the headrace to the forge. The forge itself has been lost, but its wheelpit can be identified close to the track up the valley. Large slag and waste heaps fill the valley bottom below the dam, while beside the track is a series of ruined stone buildings associated with the forge. The principal remains are of a two-storey terrace of three single-fronted cottages, two rooms deep, radically altered on conversion to a barn, 17m long and 7.5m wide. This is now represented only by the rear wall and one end wall.

Backbarrow forges (Fig 3.34)

The buildings at Backbarrow occupy an ancient ironworking site that was probably worked as a bloomsmithy long before John Machell built a weir across the River Leven in 1695 to power his new bloomforge. As claimed in 1852, Backbarrow was one of the oldest water-powered sites on the Leven, enjoying priority of water rights. At that time, it had a fall of 18ft 2in (5.53m), with a power potential of '90–100 horse' and among the buildings were a Refinery and Drawing Forge (Cumbria Record Office, Barrow: Backbarrow Sale Particulars 1852).

Throughout most of the 18th century there were at least two fineries and a chafery at Backbarrow. These forges are of particular interest in the history of ironworking, as they witnessed the first

recorded use of blowing cylinders for iron forging. The Backbarrow Accounts show that Isaac Wilkinson equipped all three forges with cylindrical cast iron bellows between 1737 and 1739 (Cranstone 1991, 88–90). After Wilkinson's departure in 1748, an anchor smithy was built in 1753, only to close in 1774 (Fell 1908, 253). As yet, there are no identifiable remains of any of these forges, despite some operation until the middle of the 19th century. Their precise location is still a matter for conjecture.

The most obvious candidate for at least one of the forges is the building latterly known as the Pugmill and used as a workshop and turbine house (Fig 3.6, E). This irregular, multiphase, two-storey building occupies the prime site for water power in the complex, as it forms the dam of the mill pond. The pond takes advantage of a natural break in the profile of the river, while a weir provides the considerable head of water alluded to in the sales particulars. It is likely that detailed archaeological investigation of the Pugmill would reveal some evidence of one, or possibly more, of these early forges.

The Pugmill is constructed of rubble with irregular block quoins and is built into the hillside and the dam of the pond. The original core is a roughly rectangular,

two-and-a-half-storey building presenting its main elevation to the south with a lean-to wheelhouse to the east. It has a half-width projection to the north, the recess accommodating the water intakes. The lower ground floor plan retains the essentials of this layout. At a later date, an extension was added to the western side. The former upper west wall was largely removed to provide through access and the western pitch of the original roof raised to allow a continuous pitch. The phasing is evident in a straight joint in the southern elevation and by changes in the roof-framing, while the differences in the depiction of this building in OS mapping between 1846 and 1888 suggest that the extension was constructed between these dates. This may accord with Fell's suggestion (1908, 255) that the forging of bar iron ceased on the site at about this time.

On the ground floor, within the fabric of the western wall and directly opposite the axle arch in the east wall, is one of a pair of large stones projecting from the wall at ground level. The alignment is unlikely to be a coincidence and these stones may well be relict evidence of the original function of the building which, if a forge,

Figure 3.34 Backbarrow Furnace: blast furnace complex from the south-west; the 'Pugmill' is prominent alongside the river at centre right (NMR 12980/12).

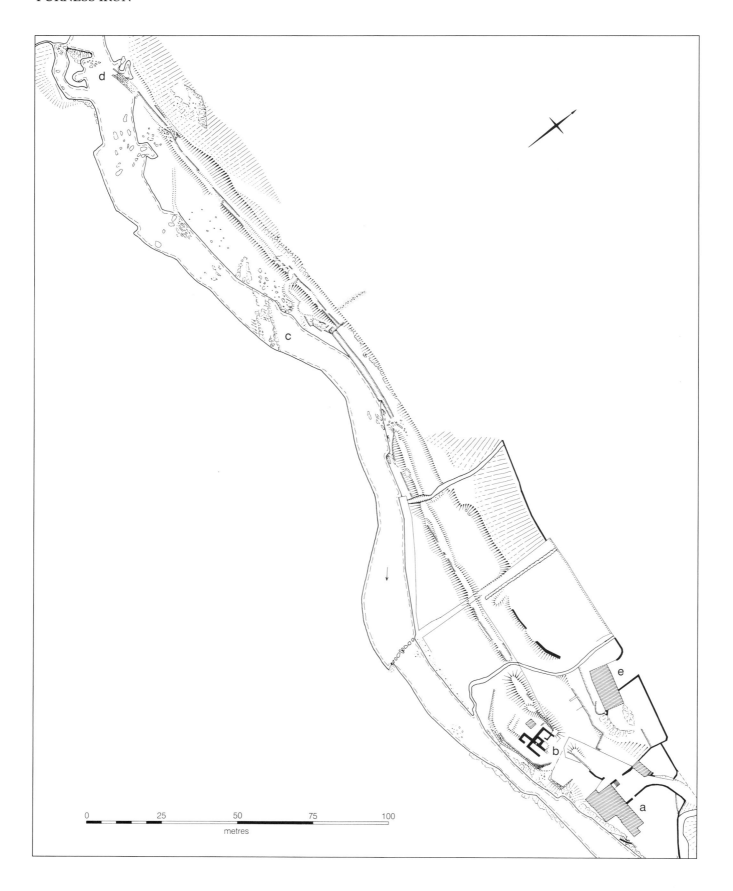

0   25   50   75   100

metres

would have involved tilt hammers with large bearing blocks and stone-based anvils. The wheel house, which occupies the south-east corner of the building, has large stone bearing blocks and bolts indicating a waterwheel some 3m wide, but this was replaced by turbines long ago.

The 1846 OS map shows a second building of similar size to the Pugmill on the riverbank immediately to the south. Its shape, with a projection at its south-eastern corner, is very similar to that of the Pugmill. It is therefore possible that this building was one of the other forges and some sub-surface evidence may survive in this location.

The Pugmill latterly operated as a hydro-electric generating station, supplying all the power required by the last phases of operation of the blast furnace. Its turbines are still used to generate electricity.

Hacket forge, Little Langdale (Fig 3.35)
Ironworking began at Hacket Forge (NY 322 030) some time between 1623 and 1630, when the ironmaster William Wright converted two fulling mills on the River Brathay to create a bloomforge. A lease of water rights obtained by Wright in 1631 from Joseph Pennington, the lord of the manor, stipulated that the forge should not be detrimental to other industries which also used the river:

> All that his Riuar or Water wthin the Manor of little Langdale commonlie called or knowne by the name of Haccat Water or Langdale Water and the banks on both sides thereof soe farre as the right of the said Joseph Pennington extendeth And also the dam and dik thereunto belonging as the same are alreadie builded erected and made upp wth libertie to pound and stay the water issueing and coming to the Forge or Iron worke there standing for making barre Iron soe often as need shall requier not hindering the water corne millne or millnes or anie the Eelearkes or Eelearke and fishinge ... for and dureing the terme of one and twentie yeares . . . (Fell 1908, 197).

After Wright left Hacket in 1633, the forge was worked by the Braithwaite and Fisher families until at least 1680 (Tyson 1989). The Society of Mines Royal Copper produced iron at Hacket *c* 1697. Their tenure must have been short-lived, however, because by 1710 the forge was in the hands of John Machell of the Backbarrow Company (Raistrick 1968, 97). In 1711 Hacket 'ceased to be a bloomery forge, but was again at work in 1713 refining pig iron and making it into bars' (Fell 1908, 198). The pig iron came from the blast furnace at Backbarrow and was brought to Hacket via Coniston Water. Although the Backbarrow and Cunsey companies rebuilt and equipped a number of forges in 1713, Hacket was not one of these; its turn came in 1715, at the same time as the two companies took out a joint lease on the site. This sequence of events suggests that the forge did not need any immediate rebuilding to allow its change of function and that the main stimulus for refitting was the joint agreement. The site was probably not used after 1726, despite being repaired in that year (Fell 1908,198). It nevertheless remained in the hands of the Backbarrow Company until 1744 and was leased by the Newland Company between 1750 and 1766.

The surviving remains comprise a well preserved leat and pond, both now dry, which extend for 255m along the river bank. The location of the forge building could not be positively identified from the survey but probably occupied what is now the site of Forge Cottage (Fig 3.35, a), a private residence, which lies at the head of the pond, on a rocky eminence overlooking the river. A conjoined group of ruined outbuildings (Fig 3.35, b), which stands on a platform adjacent to the southern side of the pond, may contain the vestiges of other buildings associated with the forge.

The leat is cut into the base of the natural slope alongside the river (in places into bedrock), while its southern side is formed by a retaining bank, which was almost certainly stone-revetted on both sides. Although long stretches of the internal face are well preserved, the external or southern side is marked only by an earthen scarp. The lower section of the leat coincides with a meander in the course of the river and its retaining wall is more robustly built to withstand erosion. The body of the wall is strengthened by another line of stonework along its exterior.

The leat was originally much shorter and in its earlier form ran from a waterfall (Fig 3.35, c), making use of the drop of the falls to create a head of water. All that survives of the original take-off is a short length of abandoned channel between the beginning of the lower section of leat and

Figure 3.35 (facing page) Hacket Forge.

the waterfall. Its retaining wall is very crudely built of boulders and is different in form from the existing lower leat, which suggests that the lower leat has been rebuilt on its original line. The earlier arrangement clearly became unsatisfactory – perhaps because of the difficulty in controlling the flow of water there – and the leat was lengthened, bringing it to a more suitable take-off point at a deeper and less rocky section of the river, where a weir could be constructed Fig 3.35, d). The junction of the two phases is marked by a stone-built step in the channel, 1.1m high.

The weir marks the extreme western end of the site. The surviving section, adjoining the northern riverbank, is composed of gently pitched, waterworn stonework. The alignment of this portion of the structure indicates that, on the southern side of the river, the weir sprang from a natural rock outcrop which juts into the river. The weir was placed diagonally across the river, which would have served the dual purpose of directing the flow towards the leat and reducing the damaging effect of floodwater upon the structure. A short channel, cut into the southern riverbank and revetted with roughly faced boulders on the south-western side, bypasses the weir. It might have been built to comply with the requirements of the original water lease to enable eels and other fish to pass up river; a similar bypass channel exists at Nibthwaite blast furnace, where a dispute over the water system and its effect on eel trapping gave rise to a court case (Brydson 1908, 99–107).

The pond, which develops from a gradual broadening of the leat, is 130m in length. The pond wall, like the upper leat, takes the form of a stone-revetted earthen bank. Two streams flow across the bed of the pond and out through two breaks in the dam wall to join the river; originally these must have added to the head of water in the pond. The westernmost of these breaks is being actively eroded by the stream and has exposed the structure of the dam wall. This shows that it has an earth core, the whole standing on a foundation of medium-sized river boulders. Such a form is consistent with documentary descriptions of using sods of earth for building and maintaining the dam walls at Cunsey and Muncaster Head (Phillips 1977a, 21).

The central sector of the pond narrows in width because the field to the north has been levelled and the resultant spoil pushed forward into the pond. This landscaping, which must have occurred after the pond had gone out of use, may have been done to create more easily cultivable land when Hacket became a smallholding. More recently, the appearance of the eastern end of the pond has been altered by the creation of a number of modern garden features, but there is no evidence to suggest that it was ever larger than its present size. A break in the pond wall, close to the head of the pond, marks the site of a sluice gate. The outflow channel has been infilled but its course is visible as a slight depression in the ground surface.

The post-industrial occupation of Hacket has removed any immediate traces of the forge and the other buildings associated with it. Adjacent to the southern side of the pond is a stone-revetted platform which stands 1.7m above the river. Upon the platform are the ruinous remains of a group of outbuildings Fig 3.35, b) comprising four compartments. The most intriguing feature is a square, cell-like structure in the centre of the upstanding remains, which has no apparent entrance. In its southern walls is a splayed vent and in its eastern wall a small aperture, inserted at about head height; its function is unknown. The buildings have been restyled on a number of occasions. Earthwork remains of further walls to the west indicate that at one time the complex was larger. These remains are unlikely to represent the forge itself – the layout would be unorthodox. It would also have had the serious disadvantage of only allowing room for a single wheel, thus negating much of the effort of constructing the water supply system. The buildings may have been ore stores, offices, or stabling.

Analogy with other sites suggests that the forge was situated at the head of the pond, close to or on the site of the present day Forge Cottage (Fig 3.35, a). The main body of Forge Cottage is probably of 18th-century date. This would fit Fell's assertion that the Newland Company gave up its lease in 1766, thus ending Hacket's association with ironworking. There is no architectural evidence to suggest that Forge Cottage was ever anything other than a domestic dwelling. This in itself is not surprising since the industrial buildings may well have become ruinous during the years of disuse, but the forge probably offered a useful supply of building stone. In 1997, the owner of Forge Cottage extended an area of hardstanding at the head of the pond, revealing thick deposits of charcoal which would also imply that the forge was situated near here. Although there is no trace of a wheelpit or tailrace – they were probably both infilled when the site assumed a domestic function – it was probably orientated east–west, continuing the line of the pond.

A barn (Fig 3.35, e) on the northern side of the pond could occupy the site of the charcoal store which the forge would have needed. Although the present building displays no features which are diagnostic of a charcoal barn, its situation satisfies all the requirements of one, and would allow gravity to facilitate the loading and unloading of charcoal.

Stony Hazel Forge, Rusland (Figs 3.36–3.39)

Stony Hazel Forge, situated on the east bank of Force Beck in deciduous woodland (SD 337 897), was the last bloomforge to be built in Furness and is unique in being constructed after the establishment of blast furnaces in the region. A pond and leat (both now dry) and the upstanding remains of the forge and a second building occupy a confined strip of land between the beck and the foot of the river terrace. Traces of further structures and a ruined boundary wall are located on the summit of the terrace, overlooking the forge.

Stony Hazel is first documented in 1664–5 as an enclosure of coppice woodland owned by the Taylor family. In October 1718 the site of the future forge was leased to Edward Robinson, Francis Chamney and Richard Herdson by Rowland Taylor and was described as ' . . . suitable and Convenient to build a Bloumery Forge Coalhouses a Dam and other Apptenances . . . ' (Cranstone 1986, 1). The business rapidly ran into trouble; in 1720 two of the lessees were forced to petition for charity after three successive fires had destroyed their main asset, the stocks of charcoal. The lease was then reassigned to William Fletcher and Richard Taylor. The relevant document describes Stony Hazel as 'one Bloomery or Iron Forge . . . with cole house or colehouses iron house and dams . . . and also one dwelling house' and ' . . . weare [and] floodgates . . . ' (ibid, 3). Fletcher and his partner did not stay long at Stony Hazel and in 1724–5, after some bargaining, the forge was jointly leased by the Backbarrow

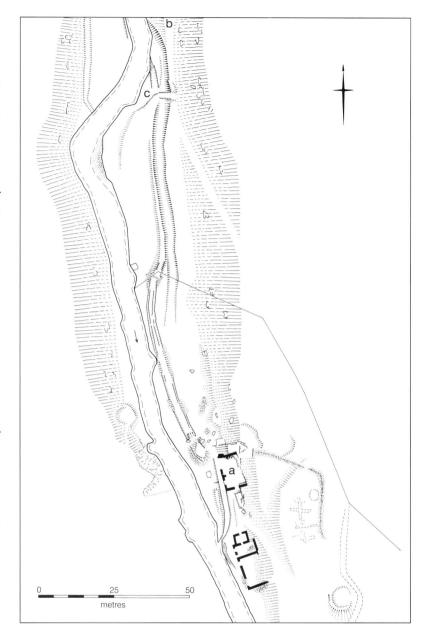

and Cunsey companies. The accounts of the two companies indicate that the forge was unused and was gradually stripped of any useful or valuable fittings. The abandonment of the site is confirmed by an entry in the Backbarrow accounts in 1743 for charcoal produced from wood 'cut down within the Compass of the Forge Ground and Dam'; the site had returned to its former use (ibid, 6–7).

The interior of the forge was first excavated in 1968–9 (Davies-Shiel 1970). By 1974, at the conclusion of his investigations, the area between the two buildings

Figure 3.36 Stony Hazel Forge.

Figure 3.37 Interior of a forge, an illustration by Denis Diderot (Gillespie 1959, plate 95).

and also the two northernmost rooms of the second building had been cleared, but the results of this work have not been formally published. In 1985 the forge was re-excavated in advance of consolidation work to the fabric of the building. Later that year, part of the dam wall and the bed of the pond were also excavated (Cranstone 1985a and 1985b).

The forge building (Figs 3.36, a, 3.38, and 3.39) is terraced into the natural slope so that its eastern side is formed from

Figure 3.38 Stony Hazel Forge: interior of the forge building, from the south (NMR AA98/08223).

hewn bedrock. The northern gable end of the forge, which is coterminous with the retaining wall of the pond, stands 2.9m high. A single doorway in the southern wall is approached by a terraceway across the natural slope to the south-east. The axles of the two waterwheels used to power the hammer and bellows would have passed through two broad openings in the west wall. The southernmost of these two openings was made narrower by the insertion of secondary stonework, while that to the north may have been enlarged after part of the building had been washed away by a dam burst (Cranstone 1985a, 4). The excavations inside the forge demonstrated that the hammer was powered by the northern wheel and the bellows by the southern wheel. In the north-eastern corner of the building were the remains of an ore bin, still containing hematite.

The most prominent surviving feature in the interior of the forge is the hearth, which adjoins the western wall. This is a rectangular stone construction measuring 2.7m × 2.5m including the external wall of the forge, which forms part of the structure. The hearth is open on three sides, the corners surviving as two freestanding pillars, each about 0.8m high. The northern opening is broader than the others and is marked by a flat sillstone set upon walling 0.2m above the present ground level. Each opening was probably enclosed by an archway, the springers of which survive above the northern opening. The excavations showed that within this larger structure the hearth proper was positioned within the southern half and was lined with brick and iron plates. The slag was tapped from the eastern opening into a small pit. Inside the hearth were traces of hematite which was also spread across the northern opening. The discovery of hematite inside the hearth and the ore bin give further credence to the historical evidence which suggests that, at the time of its abandonment, Stony Hazel had been used as a bloomforge. One structural feature of the hearth appears to contradict this interpretation, however. At the rear of the hearth is a small aperture in the wall, 0.2m square, directly above the hearth proper, which has been identified as a 'pig hole' (Davies-Shiel 1970, 30). A pig hole allowed lengths of pig iron to be fed into the hearth, a process which is depicted in an 18th-century

engraving of a finery forge which bears a striking resemblance to Stony Hazel (Figs 3.37 and 3.38). Alternatively, it has been suggested that this feature may not be a pig hole but a lever-duct to the bellows-wheel water supply (D Cranstone personal communication). Given the probable similarities between bloomery hearth and finery hearth, it is quite possible – especially given the late date of the site – that the hearth was built with more than one use in mind. No evidence for the presence of a second hearth has ever been discovered.

The second building comprises three separate rooms, the southernmost and largest of which was almost certainly the charcoal barn. The eastern wall has collapsed into the interior of the building but its northern and southern walls stand to a height of up to 3.0m. Surviving architectural detail on the western side of the charcoal store shows that it was largely open fronted, defined by a dwarf wall, 0.65m high, with an entrance at either end. Charcoal may have been loaded into the rear of the barn from the terrace above. On the northern side of the charcoal store is a smaller room with a doorway and window in its eastern wall; diamond-shaped panes of glass were found around the window during excavation. Another window and a blocked doorway are visible in the northern wall; burning of the bricks which form the sill of the window may be evidence of the series of fires during the 18th century. The presence of a finely glazed window suggests that the room may have been used as an office rather than a store. Abutting the northern side of the building is a square room with a single doorway. Its walls survive to their full height, a maximum of 2.2m, their profile indicating a lean-to roof. Unusually the room communicated with its neighbour via the window in the shared wall. The present plan of the room is somewhat different from that shown on sketch plans made during the first series of excavations (Davies-Shiel 1970, 28) and it is possible that it is a recent reconstruction.

On the terrace above the two buildings are a series of shallow linear trenches (shown as pecked lines on Figure 3.36), the result of the 1968–9 excavations. The discovery of sherds of salt-glazed pottery here by Davies-Shiel may suggest that this is the site of the dwelling house mentioned in 18th-century leases. The terrace is partly enclosed by a stone wall, now in ruins,

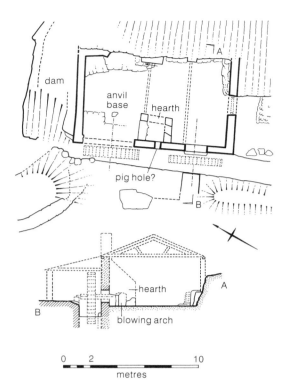

Figure 3.39 Stony Hazel: plan and section of forge building.

sandy core between two drystone walls, a form of construction which must have allowed water to percolate through it (Cranstone 1985b, 4). Although parts of the walls have collapsed, it is still upstanding to a maximum height of 1.9m internally. There were two sluices in the pond wall, one at the northern end and another at the southern, close to the forge; both are now eroded and show no structural details. The wheelpit and tailrace are well preserved despite the dam burst through the pond wall above them. The tailrace is extremely short at only 16.5m and in that distance narrows by half. Such a dramatic reduction in width must have caused the outflow to back up, affecting the efficiency of the wheels. At the end of the race, where the constriction occurs, the sides of the channel are lined with large lumps of slag rather than stone; clearly the race had eroded so rapidly that it had to be rebuilt.

The late establishment of Stony Hazel sets it apart from other bloomforges in Furness but its status in this respect may offer the key to its understanding. It is tempting to see Stony Hazel as a speculative venture by a group of individuals – maybe newcomers to the industry – who hoped to take advantage of recent developments, perhaps by refining iron from the blast furnaces, but more probably by being bought out by the Backbarrow and Cunsey Companies. Evidence for this view is circumstantial but it could account for the undeniably poor quality of construction of the pond and tailrace and most importantly, the provision of a possible pig hole in the hearth. The reluctance of the Backbarrow and Cunsey companies to re-use the bloomforge for refining iron, having gone to the trouble of acquiring the lease, is not remarkable. By 1724, the companies were already established and it was common practice throughout the 18th century for the ironmasters to retain and mothball sites to hold in reserve or to prevent competition. The lack of a second hearth is unusual but is paralleled elsewhere. It was certainly possible to use one hearth to complete the whole smelting process, as it was for refining. What is of more interest at Stony Hazel is that the same hearth was apparently suitable for both smelting and refining; it could be argued that Stony Hazel was intended as an all-purpose site.

which extends from the rear of the earthworks to the dam wall. A pitstead is situated towards the end of the terrace and a second lies on the western bank of the river, opposite the pond; these, and the numerous other pitsteads throughout the woods, are evidence of the charcoal burning carried out around the forge.

The take-off point of the leat (Fig 3.36, b), 135m north of the forge, makes use of a bend in the river to help direct the flow into the channel. The weir has not survived, but it almost certainly lay diagonally across the river, between the head of the leat and a short length of revetment wall on the opposite bank. The leat deepens progressively from north to south to a maximum depth of 1.2m and shows traces of internal stone revetment. At its head the leat is retained by a robustly built stone wall designed to withstand erosion by the river. The leat has been blocked close to this, its northern end, by a stone dam (3.36, c) and any residual flow diverted through a break in the retaining wall. This later blocking, perhaps designed to reclaim the land in the pond bay, has probably utilised the site of an earlier sluice gate.

The excavation of the retaining wall of the pond showed that it was composed of a

4

Prospect

The Landscape

The Lake District we now see is the Lake District that Wordsworth, Coleridge and their followers taught us to see – a largely natural landscape unsullied by human hand. Yet all the historical and archaeological evidence shows that Cumbria has been shaped by the human race for millennia in pursuit of settlement, hunting grounds, agricultural and pastoral land, religious observance, warfare and industry. In particular, the agricultural and industrial activities have left their widespread mark on the countryside. Wordsworth was not deliberately misleading us, however. There is unarguably a great feeling of natural space in Cumbria. He was writing at a time when the iron industry of Furness was already in decline, with only three furnaces and two forges in operation, and if it receives no mention in his *Guide to the Lakes* (compiled between 1809 and 1835) it is probably because it was genuinely not very obvious from any of the places visited on his 'Itineraries' (see Marshall 1958, 17–18). But even if it was not obvious, the effect of the iron industry on the landscape was there, and is there, to be seen.

The landscape of Furness is characterised by a number of diverse elements, but two of the most significant, the broadleaved woodlands of High Furness and the widespread mining subsidence of Low Furness, are the direct result of the iron industry. High Furness, like the Weald and the Forest of Dean, is still well wooded, in part (at least) because the iron industry needed charcoal and the ironmasters therefore promoted and protected the coppice woodlands. In a different way, the landscape of much of Low Furness, particularly the western side of the peninsula, is characterised by massive water-filled depressions, the remains of the worked-out 'sops' of hematite (Fig 4.1). These landscapes, as well as the individual 'sites' connected with the industry, are the physical legacy of ironworking in Furness. The recent revival of coppice management and traditional charcoal making in the woods of Furness by English Nature and others reinforces the historical continuum of the landscape.

The early industry

Despite the historical and archaeological work that has already been done, knowledge of the Furness iron industry in medieval and earlier times remains slight and awaits further research. Many of the field monuments relate to these periods, but until their absolute chronology is understood, there is little more that can usefully be said about them. Furness Abbey and other monastic houses were certainly involved in ironworking, but the scale of their operations, uncertain though the evidence is, appears to have been small. Some woodlands were being managed by coppicing in the medieval period, both for charcoal burning and for other woodland industries (Winchester 1987, 104–5) and, by analogy with other parts of northern England, this would be expected. How much earlier coppicing may have been practised in Furness is as yet unknown.

The introduction of the blast furnace

The development of blast furnaces elsewhere in Britain had been driven by the arms race – the ability to cast large iron guns – but that does not seem to have been the case in Furness, where ordnance and shot were a relatively late (and not enormously significant) addition to the range of products.

The bloomery was wasteful of ore and charcoal, according to 18th-century metallurgists – the hematite of Furness yielding 33 per cent of iron to the bloomery

Figure 4.1 Mining subsidence at Roanhead, from the south; the remains of Sandscale No 1 Mine can be seen in the centre foreground (NMR 12991/47).

but 46–66 per cent to the blast furnace. On the other hand, the direct process did not require the secondary process of refining to remove unwanted carbon from the iron, which was necessary in the indirect process and which consumed nearly as much charcoal as the blast furnace itself. As ore and charcoal were not in short supply that leaves capital and labour as the main economic levers of change; although the investment in each was greater in the indirect process, so was the yield, as the blast furnace produced seven times as much iron as a bloomforge in a day (Wertime 1962, 70–1). This is not to say that the bloomforges had not been successful; Milnthorpe Forge, for instance, due to careful management, was always profitable (Awty and Phillips 1980, 28).

Since demand for iron was low in the north-west during the 16th and 17th centuries, there was therefore no pressure on the ironmasters of the region to abandon the old methods. In fact the introduction of the blast furnace to Furness was to some extent driven by the outside pressure of the ironmasters from Cheshire who formed the Cunsey Company in 1711. They saw the possibilities of increasing pig iron production in an area so well supplied with ore, charcoal and, perhaps more significantly, water; lack of water to power the bellows and hammers, especially during the summer months, was one of the greatest problems for the ironmasters in the Midlands, the Weald, the Forest of Dean, and elsewhere (Wertime 1962, 110; Flinn 1959, 150–1).

All aspects of the industry – mining, charcoal burning, carriage of materials, smelting and refining – were labour intensive and labour costs predominated in the industry (Flinn 1959, 151; Fig 4.2). There was a human cost, however; the founder 'watching over the sleepless furnace himself slept "scarcely at all"' (Wertime 1962, 71). The workmen at the blast furnace were on duty 24 hours a day for several months at a time while the furnace was in blast and seem to have lived in dire conditions in the space under the charging house, as at Duddon, or otherwise in close proximity to the furnace.

Adam Smith's dictum that iron ore can be transported over long distances economically (Wertime 1962, 97) is borne out by the evidence of Furness; processing sites of both the direct and indirect processses are positioned in relation to fuel and energy sources, not the ore mines. Nevertheless, it is clear that charcoal, too, could be transported over long distances if this was unavoidable and a loss to dust of as much as 25 per cent of a cargo could be accepted. This was not total loss, however; charcoal dust could be used in the manufacture of blacking, for example, as at Newland.

There is no evidence that the Civil Wars of the mid-17th century and the lesser disturbances of the 1715 and the 1745 rebellions had any effect on the Furness industry, unlike the Forest of Dean industry, for instance, which was both disrupted and stimulated by the Civil Wars (Hart 1971, 17–19 and throughout). The major wars of the 18th century are, however, reflected in the products of Furness. The casting of guns and shot in the 1740s and around 1758–60 and 1781 was presumably stimulated by the War of Jenkins' Ear, the Seven Years War and the American War of Independence. Similarly, ballast was cast for the Navy in 1739–40 and 1755 (in the run up to the Seven Years War) but in small amounts. On the other hand, the French Revolutionary and Napoleonic Wars apparently saw no demand stimulated for Furness iron. This presumably reflects the effect of the establishment of big new coke ironworks, such as the Carron works at Falkirk. In any case the Furness industry had already entered a period of decline.

Further consideration of the well studied furnaces at Duddon and Nibthwaite, allied with further research into particular questions – such as the location and form of the forges at Backbarrow and elsewhere – will add much to our understanding of the heyday of the Furness charcoal iron industry.

Demise of the industry

The high quality of the iron produced in Furness was ultimately no guarantee of continued demand. Products with differing qualities from other, less remote, industrial areas using new techniques took away the Furness ironmasters' market. Coke smelting, steam power and the puddling process – all coal-based – were the three main technical advances which signalled the beginning of the end of demand for Furness bar iron. Furness ore was still in demand, but was smelted elsewhere or in the new coke-based furnaces of the area.

Other industries were ready to take over from iron, as reflected in the physical remains of the many iron industry sites which were converted for other uses, for example, bobbin making at Nibthwaite and gunpowder manufacture at Lowwood.

The wider economy and society

The landscape of the iron industry is interlocked with the landscape of agriculture, just as these activities were in practice interlocked with each other – individuals were involved in both, and the economics of one affected the economics of the other. For instance, in Low Furness, where arable agriculture predominated for much of the post-medieval period, agricultural wages were kept relatively high by the demand for labour in the iron mines (Tweddell 1876, 33).

At least two-thirds of the population of Furness in the early 18th century was directly involved in agriculture, which was, however, poorly developed by national standards and was not the most significant activity in economic terms (Marshall 1958, 4–8 and 11). A degree of prosperity in the late 18th and early 19th centuries is reflected in the upgrading of houses in High Furness, particularly in Hawkshead and the Sawrey area, so that they at least had fashionably symmetrical façades; this prosperity was based on the coppice woodlands rather than on sheep farming (Denyer 1991, 71–2). The value of bark is reflected in the remains of bark barns constructed especially for its storage and by the other buildings which were financed by its sale (ibid, 165). These factors are reflected in the agricultural land that was being taken over for coppice woodland, as seen for instance at Parrock Wood and possibly Bailiff Wood.

The developing blast furnace industry in the 18th century employed few directly but stimulated other industries, such as carting, shipbuilding and the coastal trade, as well as the woodland industries and mining (Marshall 1958, 16, 39). The prosperity generated remained largely in the hands of the landowners and ironmasters, but it had its effect on the landscape, not least in the creation of hamlets, as at Low Nibthwaite, or the fostering of existing settlements, as at Newland (Fig 4.3).

It is important not to overstate the level of activity in the Furness iron industry, even

Figure 4.2 Charcoal burners preparing the stack (Alfred Heaton Cooper).

Figure 4.3 Newland: the hamlet with the blast furnace at centre, charcoal barns to the right and the corn mill in the background (NMR AA98/08115).

in its heyday. Furnaces were in blast for months but could be out of blast for years while repairs were done and charcoal stocks built up; the rhythm of the woodland 'industries' was dictated by the natural cycle of the seasons. The slow pace is illustrated by this anecdote of the mid-19th century:

> A cargo of ore was loaded for Chepstow, and the captain, finding that more had been brought down to the water's edge than his vessel could take, left one wagon standing full at the stage end. He discharged his cargo at Chepstow, loaded back there for Londonderry, went thence to Bonaw, in Scotland, and brought back to Barrow a cargo of pig-iron. On his arrival he found the waggon standing full as he had left it (Tweddell 1876, 261).

The physical remains of the Furness iron industry are considerable in number and extent. Their overall spatial patterning is now broadly established but they have not yet been exploited to anything like their full potential as an 'archaeological resource'. The current series of geophysical surveys on bloomery sites represents a significant advance but more research is needed, particularly – and most urgently – in terms of selective excavation to follow up those surveys and to provide a firm chronological framework for the earlier stages of the industry.

Appendix:
Management and conservation of woodland and related archaeological sites

by John Hodgson, Lake District National Park Archaeologist

The broadleaf woodland of the Lake District is a distinctive component of the landscape and is important for wildlife and nature conservation. Its value is greatly enhanced by its historical significance as a source of fuel and other raw materials for industries that have now largely ceased and because of the abundant archaeological remains of those industries. In addition to their local importance, these archaeological remains are now recognised as being of national significance and several have been designated as Scheduled Ancient Monuments.

The Lake District National Park Authority (LDNPA) is committed to the conservation of the industrial archaeological remains described in this book, as part of the wider archaeological resource in the area. The survey work that has been undertaken by the RCHME in Furness is of great importance for locating accurately and identifying archaeological remains and for providing a wider context in which they can be understood. This will raise awareness of the value of these sites, leading to better protection and management.

Semi-natural woodland in the Lake District National Park

Major objectives for the LDNPA include the encouragement of high standards in all aspects of management, encouraging the regeneration and expansion of native woodlands, and ensuring that the full range of woodland types native to the area is represented in the National Park (LDNPA 1999). The management of woodland provides opportunities for the integration of different conservation issues, including landscape considerations, biodiversity, cultural heritage and recreation. This multi-purpose approach is reflected in the work of the authority.

Remains of past industries in the Lake District survive in different types of woodland, including coppiced woodland, areas of former coppice that are now high forest, wood pasture, conifer plantation and areas of former woodland that has now gone. The LDNPA is involved in various initiatives to enhance and extend the variety of native woodland types in the National Park. These include supporting Cumbria Broadleaves, an organisation set up with various partners in 1991 to promote the appropriate management and enhancement of broadleaf woodlands, involvement in the Native Woodland Group and provision of advice for the Forestry Commission's Challenge Fund for New Native Woodlands in National Parks.

Management of archaeological sites

Industrial archaeological remains can often pose problems for conservation because of their extent and the nature of the materials used in their original construction. In some cases the LDNPA has felt that the best course of action is to manage such sites directly, as at Duddon blast furnace. This site has been leased by the LDNPA and was the subject of an extensive programme of excavation and consolidation in the 1980s. It is now open to the public on an informal basis and an interpretation panel has been provided to assist visitors in understanding the function and importance of the remains.

Other sites, Backbarrow blast furnace for instance, may require other solutions, such as securing archaeological conservation through sympathetic re-use. In these cases, the powers available to the LDNPA as the planning authority for the National Park may be utilised. In carrying out this work the LDNPA liaises closely with English Heritage in order to secure the most appropriate conservation solution for archaeological remains.

Archaeological sites in woodland

Many of the sites described in this book are located within woodland, which can pose particular problems for management and conservation. Broadleaf woodland often requires positive management in order to maintain its intrinsic value and necessary operations such as thinning and felling, replanting and drainage can cause damage to archaeological sites if precautionary plans are not put in place. Root action, windthrow and rabbits can also damage archaeological remains. The Forestry Commission has issued guidelines on dealing with archaeological remains in woodland (1995), including practical measures for avoiding damage.

Survey is a prerequisite for successful archaeological conservation, as woodland managers need to know where sites are and what condition they are in. Archaeological information can then be included in management plans.

Archaeological sites in existing woodland should, in general, be managed in open areas with a grass or dwarf shrub cover. Grazing can be an effective means of maintaining large sites but this has to be at a level that avoids erosion. Water and feed facilites have to be positioned away from archaeological remains and any fences positioned so as to avoid damaging sub-surface remains. In smaller open areas, vegetation may need to be cut on a regular basis if grazing is not a practical option. Removal of scrub and bracken must be effected without disturbing the ground surface and rabbit damage reduced by controlling the population around sites. Felling operations must be planned carefully in order to avoid damage to sensitive remains and archaeological sites must not be used as a source of stone or other material. Timber processing and storage should be located away from archaeological remains. Damage by vehicle movement can be avoided through the use of brash matting and working only when the ground surface is dry. Trees on archaeological sites that may be susceptible to windblow can be removed and archaeological advice sought before dealing with upturned root plates. Stumps are generally left to rot in the ground, although a stump grinder can be used in some cases. New planting and restocking must, of course, avoid areas of known or suspected archaeological sensitivity.

The management of archaeological sites relating to past woodland industries, however, has to take into account the fact that they were constructed and used in woodland and should be seen in a woodland context. It may be necessary to prevent tree growth directly on such monuments but management in open spaces may not be appropriate.

Advice

The LDNPA provides advice on the adoption of positive measures for archaeological site management through responding to the consultations it receives from the Forestry Commission. These consultations involve grant schemes for private forestry (Woodland Grant Schemes) and the Forest Design Plans that are now drawn up for the Forestry Commission's own woodland. In addition, the LDNPA provides advice to landowners within the Environmentally Sensitive Area scheme, which can also provide grant for woodland schemes and archaeological conservation. Where practical conservation is required, the LDNPA can often provide grant aid for archaeological work. Awareness of these issues is crucial to the successful protection of archaeological remains and the LDNPA is active in supplying information and training to its own staff, to other organisations, and to the public.

List of References

Adams, J 1988 *Mines of the Lake District Fells*. Lancaster: Dalesman Books.

Armstrong, L 1978 *Woodcolliers and Charcoal Burning*. Singleton: Coach House Publishing/Weald and Downland Open Air Museum

Ashton, T S 1955 *An Economic History of England: the 18th Century*. London: Methuen

Awty, B G and Phillips, C B 1980 'The Cumbrian bloomery forge in the 17th century and forge equipment in the charcoal iron industry'. *Trans Newcomen Soc* **51** (1979–80), 25–40

Ballard, B 1974 *The Lakeside and Haverthwaite Railway Official Stock List and Guide*, revised edn. Blackpool: Alan Cass

Barnes, F 1968 *Barrow and District*. Barrow: Barrow-in-Furness Corporation

British Geological Survey 1997 *1:50,000 Sheet 57: Ulverston Solid and Drift Geology. British Regional Geology: Northern England*. Nottingham: National Ernvironmental Research Council/British Geological Survey

Brydson, A P 1908 *Some Records of Two Lakeland Townships* (Blawith and Nibthwaite). Ulverston: Holmes

Cleere, H and Crossley, D 1995 *The Iron Industry of the Weald*, 2 edn. Cardiff: Merton Priory Press

Collingwood, W G 1902 'The ancient ironworks of Coniston Lake'. *Trans Hist Soc Lancashire Cheshire* **53**, 1–22

— 1925 *Lake District History*. Kendal: Titus Wilson and Son

Cossons, N (ed) 1972 *Rees's Manufacturing Industry (1819-20): a selection from 'The Cyclopedia or Universal Dictionary of Arts, Sciences and Literature by Abraham Rees*. Newton Abbot: David and Charles

Cowper, H S 1898 'Excavations at Springs bloomery (iron smelting hearth) near Coniston Hall, Lancashire, with notes on the probable age of the Furness bloomeries'. *Archaeol J* **55**, 88–105

— 1901 'A contrast in architecture. Part II, the sod hut: an archaic survival'. *Trans Cumberland Westmorland Antiq Archaeol Soc* **1,** 28–32

Cranstone, D 1985a 'Stony Hazel forge: interim report 1985'. Typescript report for the LDNPA.

— 1985b 'Stony Hazel forge: second interim report, autumn 1985'. Typescript report for the LDNPA.

— 1986 'Stony Hazel forge: the history'. Typescript report for the LDNPA.

— 1991 'Isaac Wilkinson at Backbarrow'. *J Hist Metal Soc* **25**, 87–91

Crocker, G 1988 *The Lowwood Gunpowder Works*. Cartmel: R E Harvey

Crossley, D 1990 *Post-Medieval Archaeology in Britain*. Leicester: Leicester University Press.

Davies, W J K 1968 *The Ravenglass and Eskdale Railway*. Newton Abbot: David and Charles

Davies-Shiel, M 1970 'Excavation at Stony Hazel, High Furnace [sic], Lake District, 1968-1969: an interim report'. *Bull Hist Metall Group* **4,** no 1, 28–32

— 1973 'A little-known late medieval industry. Part I: the making of potash for soap in Lakeland'. *Trans Cumberland Westmorland Antiq Archaeol Soc* **73**, 85–111

— 1998 'First definitive list of Cumbrian sites of iron mines and smelt sites, January 1997'. *The Cumbrian Industrialist* **1,** 45–9

Denyer, S 1991 *Traditional Buildings and Life in the Lake District*. London: Gollancz and Crawley/National Trust

Dobson, J 1907 'Urswick Stone Walls'. *Trans Cumberland Westmorland Antiq Archaeol Soc* **7,** 72–94

— 1909 in 'Notes' section. *Proc Barrow Naturalists Field Club* **19,** 137–42

Farrer, W (ed) 1914 *Victoria County History: Lancashire Vol 8* London: Constable

Fell, A 1908 *The Early Iron Industry of*

Furness and District. Ulverston: Hume Kitchin

Flinn, M W 1959 'The growth of the English iron industry 1660–1760'. *Econ Hist Rev*, 2 ser, **11**, 144–53

Ford, J R and Fuller-Maitland, J A 1931 *John Lucas's History of Warton Parish*. Kendal: Titus Wilson

Forestry Commission 1995 *Forests and Archaeology: Guidelines*. Edinburgh

Gillespie, C G (ed) 1959 *A Diderot Pictorial Encyclopedia of Trades and Industry: manufacturing and the technical arts in plates selected from* 'Encyclopédie, ou Dictionnaire Raisonné des Sciences, des Arts et des Metiérs' *of Denis Diderot, Vol 1*. New York: Dover Publications

Hart, C 1971 *The Industrial History of Dean: with an introduction to its industrial archaeology*. Newton Abbot: David and Charles

Hendry, G, Bannister, N and Toms, J 1984 'The earthworks of an ancient woodland'. *Bristol Avon Archaeol* **3**, 47–53

Hewer, R and McFadzean, A 1992 'Iron', *in* Cumbria Amenity Trust Mining History Society *Beneath the Lakeland Fells: Cumbria's Mining Heritage*. Ulverston : Red Earth Publications, 85–106

Howard-Davis, C 1987 'The Tannery, Rusland, south Cumbria'. *Trans Cumberland Westmorland Antiq Archaeol Soc* **87**, 237–50

Jones, M 1993 *Sheffield's Woodland Heritage*, 2 edn. Sheffield: Green Tree Publications

Joy, D 1983 *A Regional History of the Railways of Great Britain: Vol XIV, the Lake Counties*. Newton Abbot: David and Charles

Kelly, D 1994 *The Red Hills*. Ulverston: Red Earth Publications

King, P W 1995 'Iron ballast for the Georgian Navy and its producers'. *Mariner's Mirror* **81**, 15–20

LDNPA 1999 *Lake District National Park Management Plan*

Lambert, J 1991 'Charcoal burners and woodcutters of the Furness Fells 1701–1851'. *Univ Lancaster, Centre for North-West Regional Studies: Regional Bull* **5**, 32–6

Lowe, A 1968 'The Industrial Archaeology of High Furness'. Unpublished BA dissertation, Department of Geography, Liverpool University

McFadzean, A 1989 *The Iron Moor: a history of the Lindal Moor and Whitriggs hematite iron mines*. Ulverston: Red Earth Publications, Northern Iron Mining Series No 1

Marshall, JD 1958 *Furness and the Industrial Revolution*. Barrow-in-Furness Library and Museum Committee

— 1984 '18th-century Duddon furnacemen – II'. *Barrow News* **12** (Oct 1984), 6

Marshall, J D and Davies-Shiel, M 1969 *Industrial Archaeology of the Lake Counties*. Newton Abbot: David and Charles

— 1971 *The Lake District at Work, Past and Present*. Newton Abbot: David and Charles.

Marshall, J D, Helme, J, Wignall, J and Braithwaite, J C 1996 'The lineaments of Newland blast furnace, 1747–1903: an historical investigation'. *Trans Cumberland Westmorland Antiq Archaeol Soc* **9**, 195–213

Morton, G R 1962 'The Furnace at Duddon Bridge'. *J Iron and Steel Inst* **200**, 444–52

Norman, KJ 1994 *Railway Heritage: The Furness Railway*. Peterborough: Silver Link

Parsons, M A 1997 'The woodland of Troutbeck and its exploitation to 1800'. *Trans Cumberland Westmorland Antiq Archaeol Soc* **97**, 79–100

Phillips, CB 1977a 'The Cumbrian iron industry in the seventeenth century', *in* WH Challoner and BM Ratcliffe (eds) *Trade and Transport: Essays in Economic History in Honour of TS Willan*, 1–34. Manchester University Press

— 1977b 'William Wright: Cumbrian ironmaster'. *Trans Lancashire Cheshire Antiq Soc* **79**, 34–45

Postlethwaite, J 1913 *Mines and Mining in the Lake District*, 3 edn. Whitehaven: WH Moss and Sons

Rackham, O 1990 *Trees and Woodland in the British Landscape*, revised edn. London: Dent

Raistrick, A 1968 *Quakers in Science and Industr*, 2 edn. Newton Abbot: David and Charles

Ransome, A 1930 *Swallows and Amazons*. London: Jonathan Cape

Ransome, A 1933 *Winter Holiday*. London: Jonathan Cape

Riden, P 1993 *A Gazetteer of Charcoal-fired Blast Furnaces in Great Britain in use since 1660*, 2 edn. Cardiff: Merton Priory Press

Rollinson, W 1996 *The Lake District: Life*

and Traditions. London: Weidenfield and Nicolson

Rose, W C C and Dunham, K C 1977 *Geology and hematite Deposits of South Cumbria: Economic Memoir for 1:50 000 geological sheet 58 and southern part of sheet 48.* London: Institute of Geological Sciences/HMSO

Satchell, J E 1984 'A history of Meathop Woods, part 2 – the middle ages to the present'. *Trans Cumberland Westmorland Antiq Archaeol Soc* **84**, 85–98

Schubert, H R 1957 *History of the British Iron and Steel Industry.* London: Routledge Kegan Paul

Smith, B 1924 *Iron Ores: Haematites of West Cumberland, Lancashire and the Lake District.* Memoirs of the Geological Survey, Special Reports on the Mineral Resources of Great Britain, Vol 8. London: HMSO, reprinted 1988 Sheffield: Mining Facsimiles

Trinder, B (ed) 1992 *The Blackwell Encyclopedia of Industrial Archaeology.* Oxford: Basil Blackwell

Tweddell, C M 1876 *Furness past and present: its history and antiquities.* Barrow-in-Furness: J Richardson

Tylecote, R F and Cherry, J 1970 'The 17th-century bloomery at Muncaster Head'. *Trans Cumberland Westmorland Antiq Archaeol Soc* **70**, 69–109

Tyson, B 1989 'Coniston forge, 14th January 1675 to 12th May 1766'. *Trans Cumberland Westmorland Antiq Archaeol Soc* **89**, 187–206

Wertime, T A 1962 *The Coming of the Age of Steel.* University of Chicago Press

West, T 1805 *The Antiquities of Furness*, 2 edn with addenda by William Close. Ulverston

Winchester, A J L 1987 *Landscape and Society in Medieval Cumbria.* Edinburgh: John Donald

Index

Page numbers in **bold** indicate
references in figures

A

Adgarley, 21
American poles and bark, 11
ancony, 3, 67
Anglo-Saxon period, 6
animal-powered pumping and
    winding gear, 21
arboriculture, 22
archaeological sites in
    woodland, management
    and protection of, 82–83
Argyll Company, 9
Ashes Wood limestone quarry,
    21
Askham, 5
Askham Park Mines, **15**
Atkinson's Coppice, 43

B

Backbarrow Company, 7–10,
    19, 47, 67–68, 71, 73, 76
Backbarrow ironworks
  anchor smithy at, 10
    smithy, 68
  blast furnace, 1, 7, 9–11, 21,
    36, 36–8, 47–8, 50–4,
    56–8, 64–5, 67–8, 71, 82
    blowing cylinder, 56–7
    closes, 47
    furnace shaft, **58**
    industry stimulates others, 80
  bloomsmithy at, 6–7, 68
  blowing house, 54
  bridge house, 54
  casting houses, 54, 58
  chafery forge, 68
  charcoal barns, 48, 61–2
  charging house, 48
  coke-fired cupola furnace at,
    58
  coke store, **60, 62**
  converts to coke, 9, 58, 62–63
  drawing forge, 68
  forge, cylindrical cast-iron
    bellows (blowing
    cylinder) at, 69
  (tilt) hammer, 71
  headrace, 48, 50

housing of workers, 66
iron ballast and cannon for
    navy cast at, 10
mill ponds, 50, 69
ore store, 48, 59–60, **60**
plan, **48**
'Pugmill', 68–71, **69**
railway line, 48, **60**
refining forge, 10, 67, 68, 79
sale details, 66
steam engine, 50, 58
turbines, 69
view, **69**
waterwheel, 54, 68, 69
wheelhouse, 69
wheelpit, 54
Bailiff Wood, 28–9, **28**, 34, 80
  charcoal-burners' huts, **29**
  pitstead, **29**
Ban Garth, 17–18
Bank End (see Muncaster
    Head)
bark
  barns, 24, 34–5, **35**, 79
  peelers, 23
  -peelers' huts, 26–9, 32
  store, 29
Barrow, 78
Barrow, railway from, 39
Barrow End wharf, 36
Barrow harbour, **5**
Barrow iron and steel works, 9
baskets, 54, 60
basket (swill)-making, 6
Beanwell, 19
Beanwell wharf, 36
Beck Leven Foot bloomery, **41,**
    42
bee bole, 31
Beela, river, 21
Bigland, John, 7
Bigland Dock, 36
Black Beck, 40
Black Combe, **5**
Black Country forges, 38
blast furnaces, 2, 3, 7, 15, 21,
    36, 46, 51–3, 78, 81
  alterations to, 56–8
  forms of, 52
  general layouts of, 52–4
  hot blast system, 58
  in Britain, 77
  lining, 57
  relining, 57–8
Blea Tarn iron mine, 17

bloomeries, 1–3, 13, 21–2, 35,
    37, 39–47, 76, 77
  description of, 39
bloomery mounds, 40, 43–46
bloomforge iron, 3
bloomforges, 3, 7, 21, 36, 40,
    46–7, 50, 67, 73, 75, 78
bloomsmithies, 3, 6, 50
blowing cylinders, 10, 58
blowing house, 51
bobbin mills, 11, 50, 79
Bolton Heads iron ore
    extraction site, 14, **14**
Bonawe (Lorn) Furnace,
    Argyll, 9–10, 47, 52, 61,
    81
  closes, 47
Boot, 39
Bordley, Agnes, 8
Bouth, near Haverthwaite,
    charcoal-burners' hut
    and pitstead, **26**
Bowness, 38
Braithwaite family, 71
Brathay, 38
Brathay river, 4, 42
Bristol, 10, 38
  forges, 67
buildings, 18, 39–40, 42–3,
    45–6, 48–56, 64, 66,
    71–3, 81
Burblethwaite
  bloomforge, 67
  refining forge, 67

C

Carnforth, 39
Carron works, Falkirk, 79
Chamney, Francis, 73
Chapel Island limestone
    quarry, 21
charcoal barns, 47–9, 58, 60–61
  descriptions of, 60–64
  in Scotland, 38, 61
charcoal
  burners, 11, **11**, 23, **80**
  -burners' huts, 26–8
  burning, 6, **11**, 23, 32–4, 40,
    43, 73, 77, 79
  carried by packhorse, 61
  -fuelled furnaces and forges,
    22, 36, 42, 45–6, 48, 54,
    57, 61, 63, 78–9, 81

charcoal (cont'd)
  industry, 1, 7, 9–10, 22, 36
  price fixing of, 9
  size of sacks, 61
  supply of, 9, 37, 38–9, 45, 50,
    59, 73
charging house, 51
Chepstow, 38, 81
Cheshire, ironmasters from, 78
Cheshire forges, 38
Christcliff, iron mines near, 17–18
Cinder Hill, 40
Cinderstone Beck, 40
clay tobacco pipes, 45
Cleator, Cumbria, blast
    furnace, 7, 46
'coal house', 45
coke industry, 11
coke works, 79
Coleridge, Samuel T, 77
Colwith Force bloomery, **41,**
    42–3
Colwith Wood, 40
Conishead Bank wharf, 36
Coniston, 14
  bloomforge at, 7, 14, 67
Coniston Water, 4, 7, 10, 22,
    27, 28, 36–8, 40, 42, 71
Cookson, Faithful, 17
copper industry, 36–7
coppice woodlands, 77–8
  take over agricultural land,
    80, 81
coppicing, 6, 11, 22, 28, 47,
    77–8
  hazel, 23
  oak, 24
Cornish miners, 17
Cotton, Daniel, 7
coupe stones, 34
'coupes', 22
  demarcated by streams, 28
Cowper, E A and regenerative
    stoves, 58
Crake, river, 10, 36, 50, 51, 67
Crake valley, 22, 36
Craleckan Furnace, Argyll,
    9–10, 47, 48
  closes, 47
Crane House quay, river Leven,
    36, **37**, 38, 39
Crew, Peter, 1
Crown Quarry, 21
Cumberland, 4, 17
Cumbria, 5, 7, 12, 14, 47, 77

Cumbria Broadleaves, 82
Cumbrian Amenity Trust
    Mining History Society
    record mines, 1, 18
Cunsey Beck, 68
Cunsey Company, 7–9, 19, 47,
    67–8, 71, 73, 76, 78
Cunsey ironworks
    blast furnace, 7, 36–7, **37**,
      47–8, 50, 67
    closes, 39
    bloomsmithy and bloomforge,
      6–7, 67–8
    charcoal barn at, 61
    dam walls, 72
    headrace, 50, 68
    housing of workers, 68
    mill pond, 68
    refining forge, 67–8
    wheelpit, 68

D

Dalton, medieval iron mines
    and mining, 15, 39
Darby, Abraham, 9–10
'deads', 15
Devil's Bridge, 38
Devonshire Quarry, 19, 21
Diderot
    on explosions in furnaces, 58
    views of blast furnaces, 51–2
    view of interior of forge, **74**
    view of interior of rolling mill
      (described), 65
documentary research, 2
    sources, 40
Domesday Book, 6
Duddon Bridge, 38
Duddon ironworks
    blast furnace, 8–10, 38, 47–8,
      50–52, **51**, **53**, 56–8, 65,
      66, 79, 82
    excavations at, 82
    hearth, 57
    shaft, **57**
    stack, 52, 55
    blowing house, 54
    bridge house, 53–4
    casting arches, 56
    casting house, 54
    casting pit, 54
    charcoal barns, **49**, 61–3, **63**
    charging house, 50, 53–4
    cottages, **65**
    forge, 64
    headrace, 48, 50
    housing of workers, **65**, 66
    open to public, 82
    ore store, **49**, 59–60, 62
    plans, **49**, **60**
    reconstruction of, **4**
    waterwheel, 49, 51
Duddon river, 4–5, **5**, 10, 15,
    38, 48
Duddon Valley, 48
Dunnerdale, **5**, 22

E

Ekman, Gustav, Swedish
    metallurgist, 3, 60
Elizabeth I, decree against
    bloomsmithies, 6
Elliscales mines, 6
engine houses, **15**, 18–19,
    20
engines
    Cornish, 17
    pumping, 17, 21
    steam, 17, 21
    winding, 17
English Heritage, 82
Environmentally Sensitive Area
    scheme, 83
Esk, river, 4–5, 45–6
Eskdale, 4, 5, 12, 14–15, 37
Eskdale mines, 17

F

Fair Hall Coppice, **27**, 28
Fearon, J, 17
Fisher family, 71
Fletcher, William, 73
flux, 9, 21, 47, 54
    fluorspar, 22
    lithomarge, 22
    slag, 22
Force Mills (Forge)
    bloomsmithy, 6–7, 67
    refining forge, 67
Ford, Richard, 7–9
Forest Design Plans, 83
Forest of Dean, 9
    slag and ore from, 10, 22
Forestry Commission, 83
    Challenge Fund for New
      Native Woodlands in
      National Parks, 82
'Fouldray headland', 4
French technical language,
    lack of, 3
    as 'high furnace', 3
Furness, meaning of, 4
Furness Abbey
    dissolution of, 6
    estates, iron mining in, 15
    after Dissolution, 15
    ironworking at, 6, 77

G

Galloway
    coast, charcoal barns, 38,
      61
    woods in, 61
Gate Crag iron mine, 17
geology, description of, 4–5
Gill Force iron mine, 17–18
Greenodd quay, 36, 39
Grizedale Beck, 22
gunpowder industry, 11, 37
gunpowder magazine, 34

H

Hacket bloomforge, 7, 14, 37,
    67, 68, 71
    charcoal barn, 73
    corn mills (corne milne), 71
    Forge Cottage at, 71–2
    fulling mills converted, 71
    mill pond, 71–2
    plan, **70**
    refining forge, 37, 67, 71
    water management system,
      68, 71–2
Hall, Edward, 7
Halton Company, Lancaster, 8,
    58
Harrison, Ainslie and
    Company, 8–10, 48, 58,
    64, 65
    install coke smelting at
      Backbarrow Furnace, 58,
      64
Harrison Coppice bloomery,
    41, 42
Haverthwaite, 24, 36, 39
Haverthwaite Heights, 29
Hawkshead, 79
Hawkshead manor, 6
Heald Wood, 23
    pitstead in, 24
Herdson, Richard, 73
High Barn Woods, **27**, 28–9
High Furness, 4–6, 11, 21–3,
    37–8, 40, **41**
    broadleaved woodlands in, 22,
      77
    housing in, 79
Hill Gill, 28
Hindpool steelworks, 21
Hoathwaite Beck, 40
Hodbarrow, 5
    Mine, 15
Holker Estate, 32, 34
Horrace packhorse bridge,
    38
Hull, 38

I

Invergarry (blast) Furnace, 7–9,
    47
Ireland, 38
Ireleth, 38, 39
iron
    ballast for the Royal Navy,
      10
    bar, 10, 67, 69, 71
      end of, in Furness, 79
      shipped, 38
    cast, 3, 8, 46–7, 64, 68
      chafery furnaces, 3
      lintels, 56
    finery, 47, 67–8
      forge (tilt) hammer, 3, 64,
      67
      forges, 3, 7, 64
      hearth, 64, 67

iron *(cont'd)*
    finished, 36
    foundries, 64
    furnace bottoms, 46
    'Lancashire forge', 3
    mines, 1, 9, 12, 15
      deep, 15
      drift, 15
      shaft, 19
    pig, 10, 37–8, 47, 56, 64, 71,
      78, 81
      produced by all furnaces, 62
    products made, 10
    puddling process, 79
    refining, 78–9
    regenerative stoves, 58
    shot cast, 10
    slag, 3, 4, 9, 14, 21–2, 35,
      38–47, 52, 68, 75–6
      heaps, 40, 42, 43, 46, 68
    smelting, 79
      furnace, 21
      with coke, 79
    transported, 37
    'white', 46
    wrought, 3, 37, 47, 64, 67
Iron Age period, 6
ironworkers, 40, 45, 54, 79
    housing, 45, 48–9, 50, 66
    involved in agriculture, 79
    wages, 79
ironworking,
    affected by availability of
      steel, 10
    effects on landscape, 77
    financing of, 9–10
    in Cumbria, 1
    in Forest of Dean, 1, 77–79
    in medieval period, 77
    in the Weald, 1, 76–77
    labour costs of, 78
    recording of, 1
ironworks, 38–9

J

joinery, 6

K

Kendal, 39
Kendall and Latham, 9
'kibbles' (buckets), 15, 17
Knight Stour partnership, 67
Knott End Wood, 30, **30**
Knott family, 10

L

Lake District, 77, 82
Lake District National Park
    Authority, 1
    commitment to
      conservation, 82
    woodland management by, 82

Lakeside, 39
Lancashire, 4, 7
Lancaster, 10, 39
Lane Ends Farm, 29
Lane Head Coppice, 43
Langdale(s), 14, 37, 43
Leeds ironworks, 38
Leighton Beck, 51
Leighton ironworks
  blast furnace, 1, 7–8, 10,
    47–8, 50–51, 58, 64
  charcoal barn, 61–2
  closes, 48
  description of working, 47
  headrace, 51
  housing, 66
  ore store, 59, **59**
  waterwheel, 51
Leven, river, 10, 19, 29, 32,
    36, 38, 48, 50, 68
  quays, **37**
Lindal, 39
Lindal Moor, 5, 38
Lindale, Wilson House, 10
Lindow, S and J, 17
Little Langdale, 40, 43, 71
Liverpool, 38
Liverpool shipyards, 10
Loch Garry, Inverness-shire, 7
Londonderry, 81
Louzey Point quay, 36
Low Furness, 4, 5, 7, 21
  iron mines in, 1, **5**, 14–15,
    18, 36–7
  mining subsidence in, 77
Low Nibthwaite, hamlet of,
    66, 80
Lowick bridge, 38
Lowwood Company, 8–10
Lowwood Gunpowder Works,
    8, 34–35, 66, 79
Lowwood ironworks
  blast furnace, 7–8, **37**, 47–8,
    50, 68
    blowing cylinder, 58
    closes, 48
  charcoal barn, 62
  forge, 58, 68
  hamlet of, 66
  head race, 50, 64
  industry, 36
  refining forge, 10, 68
lye, 24

M

Machell, James, 9
Machell, John, 7, 50, 68, 71
Margaret Mine, Lindal, 15
Marshall's boathouse, 44
Marton mines, 6
Mechlin Park mine, 17
Midlands forges, 9–10, 68, 78
Millom, 39
Milnthorpe, 21, 39, 46
Milnthorpe Forge, 78
Morecambe Bay, 4–5, 22, 36

Mouzell, medieval iron
    processing at, 6
Muncaster Head bloomery, 7,
    40
  bloomforge, **45**, 45–7
  dam walls at, 72
  equipment and materials for,
    45–46
  headrace, 46
  pond, 44–45
  waterwheel, undershot, 45–6

N

Nab Gill (Boot)
  iron mine, 12, 14, **16**,
    17–18,
  mine offices, smithy and
    store, 18
  railway, 18
National Monuments Record,
    surveys deposited, 2
Native Woodland Group, 82
Neolithic axes (see Stainton)
Newby Bridge, 36–9, **37**
Newland, 6, 8
Newland Beck, 50, 51
Newland Company, 8–9, 38,
    47, 52, 56, 67, 71, 72
  buys woods in Scotland, 61
Newland ironworks
  blacking mill (see rolling
    mill)
  blast furnace, 8–9, 21–2, 38,
    47, 48, 50, 51–2, **54**,
    55–6, **57**, 58, 64, 80
    closes, 48, 50
    hearth, 56
  blowing cylinder at forge,
    58
  blowing house, 55–6
  bridge house, 55–6
  casting house, 55–6
  casting pit, 57–8
  charcoal barns, 61, 62,
    63–4
    development of, **63**
  corn mill, 64
  cylinder bellows, 56
  furnace hearth, 53
  headrace, 51, 64, 68
  housing next to furnace, **67**,
    80
  medieval ironworking, 6
  mill pond, 50, 65
  ore store, office and cottage,
    59–60, **60**
  plan, **52**, **56**
  reefing forge, 10
  refining forge, 50, 68
  relining, 57
  rolling mill (later blacking
    mill), 50, 64–5, **64**
  saw mill, 65
  view, **80**
  waterwheels, 55–6, 64–5
    overshot, 65

Nibthwaite Company, 47
Nibthwaite Grange ironworks
  blast furnace, 7–9, **8**, 36, 38,
    47–51, 55, 79
    closes, 47–8
    hearth, 55
    shaft, **56**
  blowing house, 55
  bobbin mills, 55, 62, 79
  boshes, 55
  bridge house, 55
  cannon cast at, 10
  casting arches, 56
  casting houses, 55
  cast-iron lintels, inscribed,
    55, 56
  charcoal barn, **61**, 66, **66**
    and cottages, **66**
  mill pond, 64, 68
  ore stores, 59–60
  plan, **49**, and section, **55**
    of 1746, 51, 55, 60, 62,
    66
  quay, surviving features,
    37–8
  refining forge, 10, 51, 68
  relining, 57
  saw mill, 62, 68
  water management system,
    72
  waterwheel, 51, 55
Nielson, J B, of Glasgow, hot
    blast system, 58
North Sea, 38
Northern Ireland, 22
Norway, timber imports from,
    15

O

oak 'summerwood', 23
ore
  bog, 5, 40
  'catspole', 22
  hematite (iron ore), 5–6,
    12–13, 17, 19, 21, 36,
    38, 39, 40, 43, 45–6,
    47, 59, 60, 75, 77
  iron, 9, 12, 15, 36–7, 45, 47,
    54, 77, 79, 81
  exported, 7, 9
    to Scotland and Leeds,
    38
  extraction/mining, 12–22,
    79, 80
    engine shafts for, 15
    horse gins, 17, 20
    inclined planes, 17–18
    methods, 15
  from Staffordshire and
    Wales, 60
  movement of in tubs and
    wheelbarrows, 17
  shafts and heads, 19–21
  spoilheaps, 17–21
  transport of, 36–9, 81
  ventilation shafts, 17–18

ore (cont'd)
  miners paid by tribute
    system, 17
  stores, 22, 39, 48–50,
    59–60
  veins, 5, 12–15, 17–19, 21
Orgrave mines, 6

P

packhorse bridge, 38
  tracks, 18, 38
Palace Nook quay, 36
Parrock Wood, 29–32, **30**, 34,
    80
  charcoal-burners' hut, **31**
  pitstead, **31**
  potash kiln, **31**
peat firing at Backbarrow and
    Newland, 10
Pennington, Joseph, 71
  William, 45
Penny Bridge ironworks
  blast furnace, 8–10, 36, 47–8,
    50, 61, 68
  closes, 48
  charcoal barn, 51–2
  headrace, 50
  quay, 36
Piel Island, 4, **5**
pitsteads, 2, **11**, 23–4, **24**,
    27, 28–9, 30, 32, 43, 76
Plumpton Hall road, 38
Plumpton mines, 6
Plumpton wharf, 36, 39
potash kilns, 24–5, 32–4, 42
potash production, 1, 6, 11,
    22–5
pottery, salt-glazed, 75
Preston, 7
Price, John, 1

R

railheads, 18
railways, 17, 38–9, 60
  Backbarrow, **60**
  Barrow, 39
  Boot station, 17
  Boot to Ravenglass, 17
  Coniston, 38
  Eskdale, 10, 17
  Furness, 10, 21, 39
    Lakeside and Haverthwaite
      branch line of, 48
    Stainton mineral branch
      of, 19, 21
  Haverthwaite station, 39
  Nab Gill (Boot), 18
  Plumpton junction, 39
  Ravenglass and Eskdale,
    39
  Ulverston and Lancaster,
    39
  Ulverston–Carnforth, 39
Ravenglass, 22

Rawlinson, Job, 8
  Thomas, 7
  William, 7, 68
recording
  by Lancaster University
    Archaeological Unit, 1
  by RCHME, 1, 82
Rees, Abraham, 47, 57, 65
research areas, 81
ridge and furrow, 14, 42, 46
Rigg, Thomas, 7
Rigg family, 8
Rigg Wood, 29–32, **30**
road-based transport, 38–9
Roanhead, 5
  mining subsidence, **78**
Roanhead iron mines, Kathleen
    Pit, engine house, **15**
Robinson, Edward, 73
rolling mills, 50, 64–5
Roman period, 6
Romano-British finds, 46
Roudsea Tarn, 32
Roudsea Wood, Haverthwaite,
    24, 30, 32–5, **33**
  bark barn, **35**
  bark-peelers' hut, **25, 34**
  limestone quarry, 21
  potash kiln, **25**
Rusland Pool, 29
Rusland valley, 22

S

'sammel', 23–4
Sandys, Miles, 61
Sandys family, 6
Sawrey area, 79
Sawrey family, 6
Scotland, 9
  charcoal from, 38
sheep farming, 79
sheep grazed in wood, 29
Shropshire, 9
slate industry, 36–7
Smith, Adam, 79
soap industry, 1
Society of Mines Royal Copper,
    71
'sops', 5, 15, 77

South Cumberland Iron Co,
    17
'sow and pigs', 47
Spark Bridge bloomforge, 67
Springs bloomery, 40–41, **41**,
    42
Staffordshire, 10
  forges, 38
Stainton, prehistoric axes
    stained with hematite at,
    6, 12
Stainton with Adgarley, 19
steam power, 79
stone boundary and field walls,
    29–32, 34, 36–7, 39, 71
Stone Closes iron mine, 18–21,
    19
Stony Hazel Forge, Rusland
  bark-peelers' hut, **25**, 32
  bloomforge, 73
  charcoal barn, 75
  coppice woodland, 73
  dam wall, 74
  dwelling house, 75
  excavations, 73–6
  forge, 7, 67–8
  forge hearth, 68, 75–6
  interior, **74**
  'pig hole' or lever-duct, 75–6
  pitstead, 23, **24**
  plan, **73**
  plan and section, **76**
  pond, 73–6
  tailrace, 76
  water-driven bellows and
    hammer, 75
  water management system,
    72, 76
  waterwheel, 75
  wheelpit, 76
'stoping', 15, 18
Stour valley forges, 38
stringhearth, 3
survey
  aerial reconnaissance, 2
  Electronic Distance
    Measurement, 2
  geophysical on bloomery
    sites, 81
  Global Positioning System, 2
'swills', 26

T

tanning industry, 11
  bark for, 22, 24
Taylor, Richard, 73
Taylor family, 73
timber, shortage of, 15
timber and bark dealing, 10
Tom (Tarn) Gill bloomeries,
    36, 40, 43–5, **44**
'top-slicing', 15
Townhead, 38
Tramways, 17
transport of raw materials,
    36–9, 79
Troutbeck Park, 1
Turners Wood, 22
turning, 6, 23
turnpike roads built, 38–9

U

Ulverston, 3, 39
  canal, 10, 39
  medieval iron processing at, 6
Ulverston and Lancaster
    railway company, 39
Urswick, 5
Urswick Stone Walls Iron
    Age/Romano-British
    settlement, 12, **13**
  bloomery, 14
  iron mining, 12–13, 18

W

wagonways, 20
Wales, 19
  South, 10, 38
Walney Island, 34
Warrington, 10
Wars
  American, of Independence, 79
  English Civil, 79
  Jenkins' Ear, 79
  Seven Years', 79
water filters, 65
water management systems, 40,
    44–6, 78

water-powered bellows and
    hammer, 3, 47, 50, 54,
    57–8, 64–5
  blast furnace, 48
  bloomforges, 21, 40
  bloomsmithies, 6
  forges, 64
  waterwheels, 50–51, 58
West, Thomas, antiquarian, 13
West Midlands, iron trade of, 7,
    9
Westmorland, 4, 7
Wetherlam, 37
wheelrace, 45–6
Whillan Beck, 17, 18
Whitehaven, 10, 14
Whitehaven Iron Mines Ltd,
    17–18
Wilkinson, Isaac (pot-founder),
    8, 10
  develops blowing cylinder, 10
  fits blowing cylinders, 69
Wilkinson, John, 10
Windermere, Lake, 4, 10, 22–3,
    36, **37**, 38
winding house, 18
Windy Hills, bark-peelers' hut, 32
Woodbine Pit, Furness, 15
wood and timber products, 22,
    26
woodcutters, 23
woodcutting, 23
woodland
  importance of broadleaves, 82
  industries, 22–3, 77, 80–81
  management, 1, 6–7, 11
  tracks and paths, 29–31, 34
woodmens' families, 26
  huts, 25
woods in Scotland, 61
Woolwich, 10
Wordsworth, William, 77
Wright, William, of Brougham,
    45, 71
Wrynose Pass, 43

Y

Yewdale, 36
Yorkshire, 9